SpringerBriefs in Finance

More information about this series at http://www.springer.com/series/10282

Claudio Scardovi

Restructuring and Innovation in Banking

Springer

Claudio Scardovi
AlixPartners
London
UK

ISSN 2193-1720 ISSN 2193-1739 (electronic)
SpringerBriefs in Finance
ISBN 978-3-319-40203-1 ISBN 978-3-319-40204-8 (eBook)
DOI 10.1007/978-3-319-40204-8

Library of Congress Control Number: 2016948298

Printed on acid-free paper

This Springer imprint is published by Springer Nature
The registered company is Springer International Publishing AG
The registered company address is: Gewerbestrasse 11, 6330 Cham, Switzerland

Preface

This book is really meant to address a couple of gaps in academic and business literature.

On one side, restructuring and turnaround are topics well covered for corporates, but there is limited literature and formalized knowledge available on how to restructure and turnaround a bank or a financial institution in general. This mix of art and science is also rapidly evolving, following the recent global financial crisis and the—now well under full implementation—European regulatory regime for managing banking failures, to disconnect the link between a bank insolvency and the potential home Country's one, and to be less of a burden for taxpayers in the future. Also, the methodology needs to be clarified and differentiated as banks are just different for well-known reasons, here amply described.

On the other side, the scope and detail of the financial changes happening right now because of digital innovation and of the so-called fin-tech revolution is not well documented and ever changing—often the realm of hyper-visionaries or techno-scientist, of the booms and busts of the capital markets. This financial innovation is actually one of the main structural reasons that will make banks keep failing, even increase their rate of demise in the future, as they will be outsmarted by e-players and shadow banks, and will therefore need to restructure, turnaround, and transform, or just be liquidated—for the benefit of markets and societies as intuitively explained in the Schumpeterian principle of "creative destruction"—new life and stronger breeds are born out of death and by the reallocation of the ashes.

Building on these two gaps, this book is explaining "how to restructure and turnaround successfully a bank or financial institution" given not just what has happened, but what is going to happen in the global financial system because of digital innovation—across geographies and business models, and encompassing all main fundamental functions of the global financial system. The agenda (now still under development and with some potential future refinement) covers the topics taught by the author at similar courses held at SDA Bocconi in Milan—master in corporate banking and finance; master in corporate finance; and executive master in banking and real estate—and at the Imperial College in London (master in management—course of risk management, with cases on banking restructuring and turn around). It is also supported by the first-hand experience gained by the author as a practitioner and adviser focused on banking restructuring and turnaround topics and leading the FIG practice of one of the major consulting companies active in this area, and he is also a contributor/participant to fin-tech working groups at the WEF.

Special thanks to Daniele Del Maschio and Paolo Pucino for their support and relevant contribution.

London, UK Claudio Scardovi

Contents

Chapter 1
Creative Destruction in the Global Financial System

Abstract In this chapter, the Schumpeter's framework of creative destruction is considered and discussed on how it could apply in a more profound and novel way to the industry of the financial services and at global level, as a result of the remnants of the past financial crisis and of the profound changes introduced by quick digitization. The chapter also discusses why this "creative destruction" has so far been very limited because of the assumed principle summarized by the sentence "banks cannot fail". Actually, the chapter reviews what led to the failure of a major bank such as Lehman Brothers and what could happen if a SIFI (Systemically Important Financial Institution) were to fail, and what kind of systemic impacts could this last one bring about. The chapter is then discussing why a "bankaround" (a significant turnaround of banking) is now long overdue and almost inevitable—we are just at the beginning, in short, and not at the end of the change journey that started with the global financial crisis of 2008. The models, methodologies and approaches that will be helpful to consider to successfully face this challenge of change will then be presented and discussed in future chapters.

1.1 The Gale of Creative Destruction

According to Schumpeter, the "gale of creative destruction" describes (vividly) the "process of industrial mutation that incessantly revolutionizes the economic structure from within, incessantly destroying the old one, (and) incessantly creating a new one. This process is the essential fact about capitalism".[1] Sometimes used in a more Marxist view as reference to the intertwined processes of the accumulation and annihilation of wealth under capitalism, and sometimes as more positive view of the economic innovation cycle in business, the concept invariably mirrors the one of genetic evolution and survival of the fittest. The ones that are better fit will survive, at the expenses of the others, so as to make the overall good of species. The ones that are genetically superior will thrive and procreate and their off springs will

[1]Joseph Schumpeter, "Capitalism, socialism and democracy", 1942.

C. Scardovi, *Restructuring and Innovation in Banking*,
SpringerBriefs in Finance, DOI 10.1007/978-3-319-40204-8_1

be better positioned to dominate the evolving ecosystem, until someone stronger will show up. Life is borne out of death, and evolution out of disappearance, and innovation out of destruction.

According to Schumpeter (and to evolutionary genetics, from Darwin to Dawkins), this unavoidable process of "creative destruction" applies to Countries and economies, as well as companies and people, and even—we could argue, to the most fundamental functions that are underpinning the global structure of modern economic systems and of their financial, "heavy" plumbing.

In this handbook, we will argue that this "creative destruction" is now becoming particularly true for international and domestic financial players and for the overall main functions of the global financial system, as a new wave of disruption ushered in by digital innovation is rapidly challenging all of the major existing business paradigms, threatening the very existence—if not of banks, insurance companies and other financial main intermediary players—of their business and operating model. In banking, we will argue, Schumpeter is back for good, and the "creative destruction" has just started, bringing in unprecedented challenges (for traditional players) and opportunities (for new ones, mostly digital) that will therefore require a lot of restructuring, turnaround and transformation (and eventually, some resolution).

This handbook is therefore focused on the topic of "how to do it in banking", as the fundamental, secular challenge that started to take place in the global financial system with the crisis of 2008 is just the beginning, and we are nowhere near the end. The "how to do restructuring, resolution, turnaround and transformation in banking" (in our parlance, "how to do bankaround") is in fact neither a science nor an art, at this point in time, as limited are the real life experiences and mostly subjected to regulatory and government led/politically influenced interventions that, in the past, influenced the otherwise normal interplay of market forces). This will not need to necessarily be the case in the future, as the costs payed by taxpayers in the last few years for "bankarounds" badly planned and executed, are now leaving room for a more extensive role of the market forces: banks will be let to fail, or be restructured, turned around and transformed for good, and in a much more similar way to what is actually the normal case with a corporates.

In this book, we will therefore try to address:

- The idea and the overall logic of what is just starting to happen, commenting on how this was just waiting to manifest itself on the back of the financial crisis that started to weaken the GFS (Global Financial System) since 2008. And why banks will most likely keep failing and will need to fail in a safer way;
- The overall redesign already going on at the level of the integrated value chain of main financial intermediaries, and of banks more specifically, and how this process of unbundling and "explosion" (or "disaggregation") of the financial value chain could further accelerate, following the newest wave of digital innovation and of shadow banking that was actually helped by the wave of re-regulation;

- The expected impacts at the level of the main global functions of the GFS—the plumbing underpinning the evolution of the capitalistic growth model that has dominated the last century, and not only, and how even this functions could change through time—and with what likely "bankaround" required;
- The potential disruptions and developments (e.g. destructions and reconstructions—via a mix of creation and redeployment of bits and parts of almost exhausted business models) happening at the level of the main six global financial functions. Far from suggesting that finance will become pointless and irrelevant, we will argue that a new model of finance, maybe characterized by different roles and functions, could emerge in a novel way, potentially to the overall benefit of society (whatever the harm they could cause to challenged, traditional and incumbent financial players unable to react, change and transform);
- The basic production factor of the "old" and "new" finance, from crisis to crisis, and how they will need to be rebuilt on the basis of trust (the key component underpinning information and risk—the other main GFS's production factors), then leveraging innovative technology and artificial intelligence more than capital—but still leaving a key role to be played by enlightened and inspired management leaders;
- The best approach to move forward, taking a step back on the "destructive" part of the equation, and the best approach to safely unfold not-more-viable business model, via a mix of restructuring, turnaround, transformation and resolution (that will include also a lot of liquidation of gone concern businesses). We will dedicate extensive analysis to the different phases, their interconnection and their likely evolution within the new frame of the European banking resolution regime. Also, few specific and relevant case studies will be discussed and analyzed, with a number of open ended questions to suggest discussion;
- Far from celebrating the "post mortem" of traditional financial institutions, the transformation/innovation "challenge" that will need to be overcome. We will also comment on the "new" GFS taking shape (in terms of frame, purpose and functions). We will finally argue how the Schumpeterian "creative destruction" underway, and its evolutionary implications, driving the survival of the fittest and the disappearance of the weakest—whomever they will be, could drive to a de facto more efficient and safer GFS—better fit for the purpose of helping the global economy to prosper and grow—putting finance back to its origins and helping it regaining its fundamental trust at the service of society and people.

1.2 If Lehman Was just the Beginning

I was working as managing director and Country Head of FIG (Financial Institutions Group) for Lehman when it happened—a USD 700 Bln assets global and systemically important bank going belly up, in one of the most spectacular banking failure of recent history, almost triggering a financial meltdown that suggested the FED and the other global regulators to think twice before letting the next one go down.

Lehman Brothers, at times, had been depicted as the apotheosis of the hubris of the investment banking industry, with a great franchise and a great (individually speaking) management team just taking too much risk (in the real estate sector, mainly, and in the US) at the wrong moment (at the burst of the inflationary housing bubble driven by the FED particularly lax monetary policies post "September 11th"). It has since become a handbook case study, of the financial excesses of global banking, including "high leverage", "significant duration mismatch", "limited liquidity cushion", "excessive (structured) financial innovation", "border line regulatory and accounting arbitrage and window dressing" etc. It has also become the symbol of the nemesis biting back and coming from the predatory arrogance of the few (myself technically among them, as partner of the Devil's bank) at the costs of the so many (99 %, according to the populist slogan) left behind. It has finally become the zenith and the turning point of the crisis (the "near-death experience" of the GFS, and the moment in which central banks and governments thought better of allowing another SIFI fail and started re-regulating the industry). And of its solution, at least in the US and even if so many financial risks still remain unresolved, at least in Europe.

What if, then, the Lehman debacle was just the beginning and not the end of this "wave of mass destruction"?

What if it could be followed by a lengthy procession of further banks' failures and disappearances, even if managed in a safer and less spectacular way—"bunkerized", as it should reasonably happen, among the strict and strong walls of most recent regulations (including, ring and narrow fencing, new TLAC—total loss absorbing capital—requirements and burden-sharing/bail-in new European Union Laws)? What if the financial excesses were just a symptom (and not the real cause) of the "creative destruction" to come in the GFS?

We believe in fact that a new secular wave of disruption in the global financial industry is taking shape and will keep gaining force and momentum, driven by technological innovation and digitalization, and this will drive in turn a number of incumbents to extinction. We believe then that, even if in a safer way, a number of "old banks" will need to be let to fail—not for politically motivated purposes, or because of the clash of "larger than life" egos. But just for allowing the best reallocation of resources and the creation of a newer and better equilibrium to emerge. If this is the case, a number of considerations from the very same Lehman case could be derived:

- Lehman may have been the apotheosis of hubris. However, competitively speaking, there is an even more dangerous hubris than that for power, money and success—and that is the one for complacency in an industry under severe stress. Feeling that a status quo that has been conquered and managed for years can keep going forever is the best recipe for disaster—no hubris for change means often a lengthy but almost assured death. And risk is the salt of entrepreneurship and therefore of economic and social development;

- Lehman may have been the perfect case study of financial excesses, at a time of apparently buoyant markets and (comparatively speaking) limited innovation in the industry. But regulatory excesses could be even more dangerous, if they will prevent the market forces to do their work, allowing the evolution of the best species in an ever changing environment and extended ecosystem. Or they could allow unregulated entities to build unfair and dangerous advantages and get away with it—with new risks for the economy;
- Lehman may finally have been the proverbial nemesis, hitting the few greedy and offering a fair revenge to the 99 % left behind. But it was because of the demise of the few (many of them undoubtedly greedy—maybe as much as the remaining 99 %, if they just had the chance—but also extremely bright and talented) that an incredible damage was done to the overall economic and to the larger fabric of society—a "fair" and socially acceptable redistribution of wealth it's the duty of politics and not of economics, after all.

An even more important lesson could be derived by the demise of Lehman on 15th October 2008—a lesson better explained by way of a real episode. I was in London on that Monday morning, the day after the Chapter 11 was filed by the bank, on a late Sunday evening. Just landed at City Airport, with the usual company driver cum limousine waiting to bring me to the Lehman's head offices in Bank Street, I was asked if a 10 lb ride was OK, just before entering the black car (being a company's fleet service, cars and drivers were paid for the ride at the end of the month, directly by the bank, and guaranteed by the good name of the bank itself).

"Yes of course", was my reply, even if a bit annoyed by the strange request. If that was just the end of it! And just a normal day for a normal bank's banker!

"It would be 10 lb, paid in advance, Sir" was in fact the answer of the driver, as my word, the word of a managing director of Lehman Brothers, once one of the oldest and best reputed investment bank at global level, was not even worth the credit risk on a ten pounds ride to Bank street, with a maturity time of few minutes.

That was really what was left of Lehman Brothers, after its bankruptcy and its unprecedented loss of face: a major dispersion of the values built along with its reputation, including the financial one (linked to its creditworthiness and to its ability to keep trading on the main capital markets), the intellectual one (linked to the teams of talents that were all now ready—or better forced—to leave, to take up the first job offer available, no perks attached) and the franchise one (linked to its brand value and its portfolio of clients' relationships).

1.3 The Phoenix

The Lehman bankruptcy may have been the zenith of the global financial crisis, with wide ranging impacts that took most economies many years to digest. Following the Lehman debacle, an almost complete freezing of the monetary markets created serious liquidity constraints and spikes in the cost of financing for major banks, whilst others were completely cut off the debt market. Many global financial institutions were therefore forced to request the help of the State—the savior of last resort, with some of them being nationalized, some others rescued via mergers and partially liquidated via the creation of non-core units to be winded down in a safe way.

The following hangover on the public debt market then threaten the solvency of entire Countries and, at some point, even the disappearance of the European monetary union, as the risks of insolvency moved from the private to the public sector, because of the expensive "bail-outs" operated by few governments and the fundamental roles healthy banks play for the placement and negotiation of public debt bonds. Finally, a wave of re-regulation started taking shape, and is still unfolding as we write, requiring far more regulatory capital, higher liquidity ratios and less leverage and lots of compliance, therefore putting further pressure on the profitability of the overall global system, with an heavier weight assigned to systemically important financial institutions (SIFI).

We believe that, far from fully stabilizing the global financial system, the new wave of regulations will further weaken the competitive position of regulated financial intermediaries, limiting their chances to effectively react to the threats coming from "shadow banking players" (e.g. non regulated quasi banks) and "digital players":

- Shadow banking players, including private equity and debt funds, pension funds, sovereign wealth funds and other investment banks or broker—dealer organization and investment or trading vehicles designed and acting "just" outside the borders of regulation and therefore playing in the GFS's "shadow"—exploiting a competitive advantage also stemming from their being unregulated;
- Digital players, including direct lenders and fund raisers, providers of new payments systems or insurance brokers, acting within or (more often) outside the borders of financial regulation and competing on specific business and operational propositions built on the basis of the opportunities offered by new digital technologies and not only so as to subvert the traditional status quo and steal a share of revenues.

Shadow and digital players (sometimes with single players blurring the boundaries and competing on both fronts) will keep challenging the traditional financial institutions and will most likely provoke major disruption in the prevailing business and operating model of the industry. They could even end up challenging the main global functions—or reinventing some of the most very basic and traditional offerings of investment and commercial banks, insurance company and asset managers.

It follows then that banks will keep failing, and maybe at an even increasing rate—as the digital revolution of the global financial system fully unfolds. And, because of Schumpeter, they will need to do so, even if in a more orderly way, for the overall benefit of the economy and society at large. With some of them able to reborn from their ashes (maybe embracing innovation and digitalization in a more effective way), and some others just destined to disappear and be un-winded in the safest way. Should this be the case, we may conclude and summarize, at this point of our discussion, that:

- The recent wave of banks' failures, following the global financial crisis started in 2008 (some of them followed by liquidation, and others by restructuring and turnaround) have represented the apex for the last 50 years, but that may not be the end of the story, as a growing number of failures will become the norm;
- As we are just at the beginning of the banking crisis restructuring, resolution, turnaround and transformation journey, we may assume that the continuous financial market turmoil is more of a symptom than the cause of a more profound structural malaise of this global industry;
- Schumpeter's "creative destruction" cycle will be more and more present in the global financial system, for the public good—as it was maybe constrained by the Rule of Law and by some bygone misconceptions summarized by the old "banks cannot be let to fail" paradigm;
- It follows therefore that the Legislative framework and the evolving public and private approaches (from politicians on one side and managers and practitioners on the other side) will need to evolve quickly and effectively, to allow banks to fail more openly—and in a safer and more efficient way—in the future.

1.4 Why Banking Is Different

"Is restructuring and turnaround, or even resolution and transformation, something really new or just one of the oldest job in business and economics—as, since the beginning of competitive markets and free enterprises, so many companies have prospered but at least as many have gone under at some point of their lifetime?"—an external observer could reasonably argue. "Is banking and global finance so different, at the end of the day, if we leave aside the regulatory staff?". Or it's just a bit of a fashion of the day that will quickly disappear?

Indeed, we believe that restructuring and turnaround in banking is different, and sometimes more of an art than a science, if not a religion—with its paraphernalia of rituals, dogmas, saints and devils, and the lot of faith it normally requires, particularly during the first week-end after the outing of a critical crisis. As an art, it is also a less developed one than restructuring and turnaround for corporates, as it did not start and was not developed and nurtured by the credible threat of death (because of the "banks cannot fail" dogma).

Just to recollect briefly, there are four main reasons usually mentioned in literature that can explain why banks have traditionally not been allowed to fail (and thus merged with others or bailed out by the State:

- Politicians and regulators want to avoid the systemic "domino effect", as banks are heavily interconnected among each other and the failure of an even small one could lead to the demised of many other and of even much larger ones (this is referred as the "Herstatt risk", after the demise of a local German bank that played just like that—as the first piece of a domino). And the Lehman case is also another point in case—with the money market freezing completely after the demise of the big US investment bank;
- They also strive to maintain "stability" in the expectations and risk appetite of consumers, as banking crisis tend to generate widespread panic ("bank runs" by customers asking back their money, even if not directly financing the bank but just administered or managed by it). In fact, any robust "bank run" will lead inevitably to the illiquidity and then insolvency of a bank—no matter how well capitalized and profitable this is, because of the inherently unavoidably high equity multiplier used in the banking industry (the bank lends on the basis of a multiple of its equity—be it 5 or 50 is relevant up to a point, as even in the first case a robust bank run will show that the equity is not enough to refinance to maturity the longer term dated loan portfolio). Also, panic and bank runs tend to be "epidemic", propagating in a pandemic way and often unreasonably across markets and countries because of the "animal spirits" very keen and sensible on the matter of the "sanctity of people's savings" (also because of the obvious political implications of this);
- They also wish to avoid systemic effects, as the failure of the banking system deflagrate naturally with deep and long lasting impacts on the "real economy", impacting all kind of public and private sectors and leading to multiple market failures. As the lending supply dries up, profitable corporates start going bankrupt because of their inability to refinance themselves even if their fundamentals are solid, with people defaulting on their consumer loans or mortgages for the same reasons, and even public Institutions;
- Finally, they also want to avoid major disruptions in the working of the economy coming from the failures of some fundamental "utility function" played by financial intermediaries, such as ensuring the smooth and efficient/effective running of the payments and settlements systems. If it breaks, it could grossly impair the ability of the economy and society to retain some normal functioning of the most basic day to day activities.

1.5 If a SIFI Were to Fail

Let's take a further look and consider if not a small, provincial bank, but a SIFI (Systemically Important Financial Institution—a quite sizeable bank with businesses spreading globally and well connected with most of the international financial markets) would happen to fail, and with what kind of interlinked, sequentially driven by cause-effect, almost instantaneous and potentially destabilizing consequences. In summary:

- As an almost immediate effect, we would register the widening of interbank rates and spreads (because of the "adverse selection" problem—I don't have full visibility, therefore I do not trust anyone; and because of the globally and digitally interconnected money markets, this sentiment would be reflected in real time and across all the main participants in the short term lending market—from the overnight/tomorrow next on);
- We would then see the "liquidity tensions" leading to "fire sales" of more or less easily marketable assets, with greater and greater discounts as these super marketable assets are used up, as buyers become increasingly scarce and worried. Liquidity risk would then translate into solvency risk, as greater and greater losses are experienced via these "forced sale"—therefore biting back the liquidity situation, but also in turn the profit and loss account, and therefore the regulatory capital and thus the solvency ratio of the bank, spreading the issues to other banks in a pandemic scenario leading to the feared "domino effect";
- The solvency issues would also, almost immediately, be reflected into a "credit crunch", as the lending supply dries up—credit is just not available, not even at very high interest rates. Banks will need in fact to beef up their regulatory capital available and deleverage and de-risk their balance sheet, thus reducing revenues that, given the quasi fixed cost structure, will in turn imply a loss in the income statement;
- As the credit supply dries up, the illiquidity and then insolvency rate of corporate (mostly) and retail clients increase, as they are unable to refinance their balance sheet and are forced to further "fire sales", at deeper and deeper discounts. Recession then hits the overall economy, and banks experience even higher losses on their credit exposure and further tightening on the funding markets (for both their equity and debt needs);
- As a number of "safety nets" are thrown by governments and quasi-public institutions to just avoid the complete meltdown of the international financial markets and of the overall global economy, most of the issues get transferred from the private to the public domain, at the expenses of taxpayers. Even worst, the scale of the debt and equity (usually sub or non performing—sometimes referred as "toxic assets") transferred to the governments is just so large that a public debt crisis is then ignited, with looming interest rates required to serve the outstanding public debt issues and the spread between the better and worst positioned Countries widening at an accelerated pace, potentially leading to the insolvency of one or more Countries and to a number of "bail-outs" financed by international Institutions, often acting in conjunction, such as the IMF, the World Bank and the EU/ECB as in the case of Greece in 2013–2014;
- For the remaining, still solvent but increasingly debts-burdened Countries, a number of restrictive fiscal policies are enacted, with cuts to the welfare and other discretionary expenses and investments, and (consequently) higher taxes. The combined effect being an even lower growth rate for the economy, and further bankruptcies of companies and consumers heavily related to or reliant on public finance;

- Apart from restrictive fiscal policies (again acting as a constraint on the growth rate of the economy), a number of expansive monetary policies would then also usually be put in place, with record low interest rates set by the relevant Central Bank (even negative, as recently experienced) and greater and greater nominal amounts of money being digitally printed—a "quantitative easing" that should lead in the long run to an higher inflation or even hyperinflation, ultimately wiping out most of the value attached to fixed income denominated public and private debt, and further impacting on the real purchasing power of people;
- In parallel to these, a number of restructuring situations would pop up in both public and private realms, with huge negotiating costs, increasing frictions in the markets and further situations of distress being nurtured by the unfolding of specific, major restructuring dossiers. A loss of faith in the markets would also usually follow suit, as some of these restructuring cases would be managed "off" the market, for industries serving strategic purposes, companies that are big employers or are now ending up being owned by banks;
- As some more or less radical form of social and political unrest would also likely follow, we could experience further destruction of value, as the normal working of markets are severely impaired. The rule of Law, the principles of free markets and international commerce and even the entire fabric of society could get potentially questioned. Social unrest and change in governments, followed by populist parties usually taking the rein after deeply contested elections, would further deepen the economic loss experienced;
- As populism and autarchy follows, a number of competitive devaluations could then develop, leading to "currency wars" and also to the break-up of existing currency unions/single currency development projects and international trade agreements. Most of the Countries will try to "beg their neighbor" with these devaluations aimed at increasing exports and at importing new (even if low value) jobs, with an unclear net result on the purchasing power of their people, as most of this growth is sterile and subject to monetary illusion—you work more and have more paper money, but you purchasing power is at the end the same;
- Finally, the collapse of international commerce, the development and exportation of dreadful cycles of hyperinflation, stagflation, public debt consolidation or denial could lead to increased political and military tensions in the global arena, with regional insurrections, sectarian terrorism and potentially a major full-scale war, where the rule of the strongest is used to settle things, further destroying economic value (even for the final winner, no matter how much value it will then be able to capture from the loosing Countries), not to mention the cost of lives for all parties involved—increased by malnutrition, the spread of viruses etc.

In summary, if a SIFI where to fail, you would want to know how to be able to avoid all this, limiting the negative impacts at the earliest stages of this chain reaction. You would definitely want to do "whatever it takes" (just to mention the famous sentence pronounced by Mario Draghi, Governor of the ECB, at the zenith of the European public debt crisis) to avoid all this, and get back to normal, in the shortest possible time, limiting the overall costs (potentially not just financial, as we have seen) for the global economy and overall society.

1.6 If a SIFI Needs to Fail

Indeed, banks, including major ones and even SIFI, in many instances will need to fail—not just because they deserve it, but because it may represent the necessary evil component that ensures the "creative destruction" that brings about the development of the economy and, in the long run, the best allocation of scarce resources globally available across this and other industries. However, as we all agree that banks are a different kind of animal because of the systemic and utilities implications just commented, we also need to make sure they will be allowed to fail in a safer and well controlled—if not more effective and efficient—way in the future.

Maybe even more importantly, we need to make sure that their restructuring and turnaround can be effectively carried out, so to minimize the number of actual and full bankruptcies cum liquidation happening, and to maximize the chances that the bank being restructured and turned around will not transform itself into a zombie, scaring investors away from that market, and without the benefit of the reallocation of resources coming from the full liquidation option. Restructuring and turn around can in fact be a much more delicate task to perform than in other industries and for several pragmatic reasons:

- From a time perspective, a bank run could deplete the stash of cash accumulated by a bank in a matter of few days or even hours, should the ensuing panic generate a bank run by deposit holders. As explained, the simple rumor of a bank being bust (just because credible and believed by customers, even if totally not true) could bring a bank to a liquidity crisis, then to fire sales and then to insolvency as a self-fulfilling prophecy;
- From a cash perspective, a bank—differently from a normal corporate—is built on finance and finance is its very core business, as immaterial as you could get. It follows therefore that cash is relevant, but needs to be analyzed in a different way, as it is also one of the core products of a financial Institution. And, differently from a corporate, the cash dimension of a bank needs to be considered at the light of its leverage, because of the credit multiplier that is at the basis of banking and that makes this all more risky to be managed;
- From a debt perspective, the reasoning is very similar, as money and loans are one of the core commercial products that critically contribute to the interest margin—the most important revenue generator of a universal or retail/commercial bank—the most basic business of a bank being, at the end of the day, buying money and selling money, at a spread. Just reducing debt would therefore means to reduce the volumes intermediated and therefore to kill the revenues, with obvious impacts on the viability of the business;

- From a cost perspective, a quite efficient bank can run on a cost to income ratio of 50–60 %, of which a good two thirds are easily attributable to personnel costs. The limited scope for cost cutting on the non-HR expenses is then matched by the possibility that a reduction in operating costs is overcome by the higher costs in the costs for the operational risks. During an economic recession, it is also not unusual to have the cost of credit risk (e.g. the losses experienced on outstanding loans) higher than its total operating costs of, therefore making their optimization, if not pointless, at least much less effective;
- From an asset perspective, a bank's balance sheet is characterized by their almost dominant intangibility (e.g. leaving aside few real estate and IT assets), most of the goodwill retained by a bank is linked to its brand equity value and commercial franchise—a synopsis for the credibility of a bank, where almost everything is built on reputation and trust—and capitalized as goodwill. As intangible they are, these assets tend to fly and lose their value quickly in the case of a crisis, as the story of Lehman's debacle shows;
- From a responsibility perspective, a bank tends to fail for mistakes and the ill judgment of people and top managers often gone long time ago. As it is quick to get further revenues from new loans, it takes also a bit of time to fully manifest the full costs associated with their consequential credit losses—because of the time lag between origination and the beginning of the sub and non performing phases (particularly for the loans that are interests-only with all of the notional left for the maturity date—a kind of jack in the box surprise);
- From a governance perspective, a bank tends to get mixed up in a number of private and public dimensions, because of their specific relevance for managing the economic cycle of territories and Countries and therefore the political cycle (with banks offering easy loans on the cheap during the election time, it's easier for the political party at the helm to be re-elected, with the bad loans potentially coming out just few years later, maybe at a point where another Party has just taken the lead: thus the sensitivities on banking…);
- From an international perspective, finally, even a small and uneventful bank can have larger and larger impacts, because of its interconnectedness with the system that spans across the monetary market, the debt one, the payments and settlements systems and so on, not to mention the damage to the credibility of the overall banking system, should a single bank default and cause depositors to lose their savings.

The real challenge is therefore not to avoid absolutely and "at all costs" the demise and failure of a bank, but to maximize the chances of its successful restructuring and turnaround—no matter how brutal and drastic could this be. Or to make sure that, should all these attempts fail, an effective liquidation plan can be put in place and executed smoothly, transparently and in a quick and competitive way to recover as many resources as possible.

In Figs. 1.1, 1.2, 1.3 and 1.4, we have then summarized few of the most relevant banking failures that took place since the beginning of the global financial crisis of

Banking failures: most notable cases from recent past
Bear Stearns and Merril Lynch

Player	The Rise	The Fall	Aftermath
Bear Stearns	• Leading player in the CDO business • Performance driven through **high leverage —10x to 35x the investment** • Leverage obtained through **short-term repo**, with CDOs pledged as collateral to other CDOs • CDOs achieved **returns between 15% to 23%** • **CDO-squared** increased exposure to subprime	• More than **$16bn losses** only from CDO business in 2007 • **AUM almost halved in 10 months** (reduced to $90bn in January 2008) • **Investors' run** —one hedge fund **pulled $5bn in a day**	• **Bear Stearns acquired by JP Morgan** with the support of FED and creation of a vehicle (Maiden Lane LLC) with $30bn troubled assets • Bear Stearns business model based on **very thin fundamentals**: no diversification, extreme leverage, weak funding structure
Merril Lynch	• **Strong growth in FICC (+40%)** - $5bn in 2004 to $8bn in revenue in 2006 • Mounting exposure to **mortgages and ABS** —securitized a total of **$200bn in 2006-2007** • **Acquisition of First Franklin Financial Corp** in December 2006, in order to access the entire mortgage value chain	• **$24.7bn loss** in CDO and subprime in 2007 • **$37.9bn loss** in 2008 • Growing reliance on **short term borrowing —$460bn average repo financing** only in the year 2007	• In January 2009, **Merrill Lynch was taken over by Bank of America**, which officially took place in January 2009 • Failure in properly appreciating the **amount of accumulated risk** allowed the situation to grow out of control and proved to be deadly for Merrill Lynch

Fig. 1.1 Banking failures: most notable cases from recent past. *Sources* "Better Banking" (2013), Annual Reports

Banking failures: most notable cases from recent past
AIG and JP Morgan

Player	The Rise	The Fall	Aftermath
AIG	• AIG pursued a strategy of monetizing its AAA rating and slack capital requirements by becoming a **derivative counterparty** • Its portfolio reached **$2,700bn in notional assets** in September 2008 • At the end of 2007, AIG had **direct exposure to mortgage-related assets of $140bn** and **$25bn to Alt-A subprime**	• **$24.5bn loss reported** on 10 November 2008 • **$99bn all-time record loss** posted for the year 2008	• **FED granted a $123bn emergency loan** between September and October 2008 • Maiden Lane I and II created to absorb **$70bn of AIG troubled assets** • About **$182bn of taxpayers' money** were used in the rescue package • AIG deeply **underestimated the implicit risk to realize small fees**
J.P. Morgan	• The Chief Investment Office (CIO) was established in 2005. In 2012, its **portfolio reached the size of $360bn** • Historically focused on a "short" High Yield position, changed its strategy to **balancing short and long positions** in January 2012 —exposure to High Yield tripled to reach $157bn	• MtM losses in January 2012 amounted to $100m • **$6.2bn MtM losses** were recorded by the end of 2012. JP Morgan was further **fined for $1bn** for violations to securities law	• **CIO risk management system completely revised** • The management wanted to reduce their risk profile with the strategy change, but **poor understanding of risk convergence** led the CIO team to huge losses

Fig. 1.2 Banking failures: most notable cases from recent past. *Sources* "Better Banking" (2013), Annual Reports

Banking failures: most notable cases from recent past

Barclays and UBS

Player	The Rise	The Fall	Aftermath
Barclays	• In the end of the 1990s, Barclays founded its new investment banking arm **BarCap**, focused on loans, bonds, and derivatives • Through an aggressive investment activity, BarCap grew from an operating profit of £575m in 2000 to £2,216m in 2006 —**BarCap accounted for 30% of total Barclays operating profit**	• **£7.3bn forced recapitalization** in 2008 • Its AM[1] subsidiary **BGI sold to Blackrock to cash in.** • **£2bn provisions** for PPI[2] redress • **£850m provisions** for products misselling	• **Top management dismissed** in mid-2012 • In the mid-2013, the regulator identified a **£12.8bn shortfall in Barclays capital** • **Structured Capital Market division is shut down** —contributed £1bn revenue • Old management adopted a too risky strategy, but **Barclays was quick to react and thus survived the storm**
UBS	• In 2005, UBS decided to push in fixed income and **started bulking up in the exact areas that suffered the most in the period 2007-2009** • Simultaneously, **UBS focused its strategy on franchise and revenue potential**, rather than intrinsic potential and risk management	• **CHF13bn forced recapitalization** in 2007 • **CHF16bn right issue** and **CHF6bn convertibles** in 2008 • **Sale of CHF60bn subprime assets** to Swiss state	• **UBS share price lost 80%:** from CHF80 in 2007 to CHF15 in early 2013 • **Investment banking reduced more than 5x** • A deficient governance structure allowed the risk to balloon in UBS growth strategy.

1) Asset Management. 2) Payment Protection Insurance.

Fig. 1.3 Banking failures: most notable cases from recent past. *Sources* "Better Banking" (2013), Annual Reports

Banking failures: most notable cases from recent past

Northern Rock and Bankia

Player	The Rise	The Fall	Aftermath
Northern Rock	• **Northern Rock grew 5x in 10 years** — between 1997 and 2006 customers loans grew from £13bn to £87bn • Securitizing more than half of mortgage book allowed to **grow regulatory capital 1.4x only** • In 2007, the bank was writing **20% of UK mortgages** and growing at 40% per year.	• **Market funding dried up** and the bank searched for government help. • However, **BBC leaked details** just before the government could intervene	• The information spread panic and a **bank run** was the immediate effect • No investor was found and **the bank was nationalized** in February 2008 • Northern Rock represents a clear example of the effect of aggressive financial strategies paired with no risk management
Bankia	• Bankia-BFA was formed in July 2010 by the **merger of seven Spanish saving banks** • In July 2011, Bankia was successfully floated on the stock exchange, with a **total market capitalization of €6bn** • The bank was **heavily exposed toward real estate** —i.e. one of the biggest of the seven banks had c.70% real estate in its loan portfolio	• In May 2012, the Bank reported a **loss of €4.3bn** • Between May and September, the state offered Bankia **almost €9bn of capital injection** • **Net loss of €21bn** posted in February 2013	• **Bankia shares dropped by -99%** - from €45 at flotation, they reached €0.5 before the stock was excluded from the market • **€19.5bn of troubled assets** transferred to SAREB, the national bad bank • The case of Bankia shows how the slow and sloppy response of the authority to the crisis was not capable of controlling it

Fig. 1.4 Banking failures: most notable cases from recent past. *Sources* "Better Banking" (2013), Annual Reports

2008, with the different typologies of the causes that brought to their crisis, and then some considerations of what followed, as solutions and implications of the situations.

1.7 The Beginning of a "Bankaround"

This is not the end of a negative cycle started with the subprime loans of early 2000. And Lehman was maybe not the zenith of the nemesis to follow. Banking restructuring, resolution, turnaround and transformation will need to become the norm, rather than the exception, because of the supremacy of Schumpeter's creative destruction, and because the banks, regional and global likewise, will get more and more into trouble, and for a number of structural reasons that is worthwhile to recap:

- Digital innovation is everywhere and will lead non-banks (or shadow-banks) new players to compete effectively at all levels, including product manufacturing, distribution and infrastructure services; and across all of the fundamental functions performed by the global banking system (e.g. providing lending and other sources of equity capital, via P2P lending and crowdfunding for example; or payments and settlements, via new digital circuits and potentially involving new crypto currencies run on distributed ledgers; or covering risks in new and more efficient ways pooling and sharing via the web multiple sellers and buyers);
- Shadow banking is developing at the borderlines of existing regulations and is becoming more difficult to identify and monitor, let alone supervise. And as it is often more profitable than the re-regulated banking business, is getting stronger and stronger (but not necessarily healthier and safer). As it gets potentially destabilizing, it will threaten existing banks not just in terms of a fiercer competition, but also because of the potential impacts coming out of a major failure of few shadow banking players;
- Whilst re-regulation is fierce, it does not necessarily imply a safer banking system, as it pushes for stronger and stronger balance sheets but negatively impacting banks' profitability. For sure, it is pushing for more red tape, and an increasingly unmanageable amount of compliance, that increases the cost structure of a bank and, putting more and more constraints on its business and operating model, makes it even less apt to react and change. Also, the amount of fines imposed to banks has been skyrocketing to unprecedented levels, sponsored by the political and media driven back lash that followed the global financial crisis. This in turn is also undermining the reputation and credibility of banks (not to mention the capital base), with significant and durable negative impacts on their goodwill—thus making more difficult their day to day business and weakening their pricing and market power, both on their liability and asset management side;

- Finally, increasing geopolitical risks are continuously resurfacing, with impacts rapidly transmitted across a more and more interconnected globe: from the greater China—pacific rim region, to the middle east—to Latina America and the US and Canada to old Europe and Africa…everything is interconnected and usually banks gets burned in a matter of hours if anything negative happens (let it be the volatility in the oil price, a terrorist attack in Europe, a new war in the Middle East, some social turmoil in Asia etc.). As global "bad news" harms banks' profitability, local "balkanization" or regulatory rules (higher finishes) also drive the higher costs of businesses and investments required to manage with an increasingly hostile environment.

In short, the imperative for a rapid and significant transformation in the GFS is clear and multifaceted. And it has a number of perspectives, from clients expectations to politicians demands and regulators requests, from business model and competitive positioning to operating model and cost structure, as shown in Fig. 1.5.

As the "bankaround" (the restructuring, resolution, turnaround and transformation of banks) will gain urgency and relevance, top managers, practitioners, advisers and regulators will need to understand and learn more on what it really takes—as a number of new competitive invariances will be built out of this secular change, and a new breed of leader will emerge as most competitive survivors driving new waves of sustainable value creations.

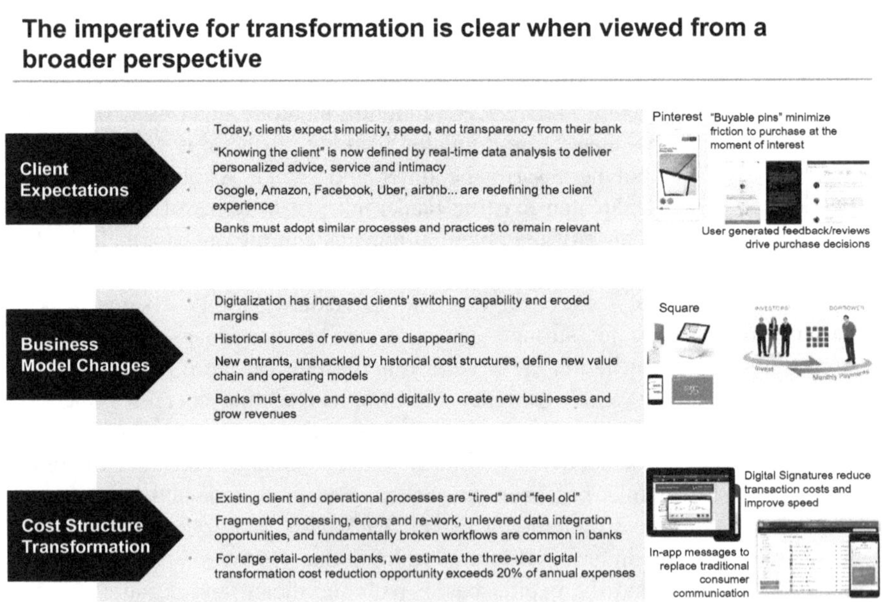

Fig. 1.5 Imperative for transformation is clear

1.8 Lehman Brothers, the Long Short

Back in 2007, Lehman Brothers was one of the most admired and envied global investment banks, with one of the best FICC franchise (Fixed Income Currencies and Commodities) and was among the top 5 American investment banks—fifth at the time, after Goldman Sachs, JP Morgan, Merrill Lynch and Citi, but with an ambitious plan to take over the top spot in few years, also thanks to its aggressive use of principal investing activities. It also had one of the most trusted CEOs at its helm, Dick Fuld—a navigated veteran, nicknamed the "gorilla" for his energy and charisma and perceived (and mentioned by The Economist) as the safest pair of hands on Wall Street (as he had survived a number of banking crisis before that, from the LTCM debacle to the Russia and Asian crisis in the '90s). Then, after reaching an high point price of USD 80+ per share in June 2007, the bank went down to zero and to its final collapse in little more than a year, potentially putting at risk, in October 2008, the overall stability of the global financial system—with frozen money, dislocated credit markets and panicking "flight to quality" of investors of all kinds across the world.

What happened during those 14 months, and was all the action and the mistakes played there, or the seeds of the Lehman disaster had been planted well in advance?

In fact, it all started at least five years earlier, in 2003 and 2004, when the bank, in the wake of the United States housing bubble, acquired many mortgage lenders and originators (not just in the US but globally), and including subprime lenders BNC Mortgage and Aurora Loan Services, which specialized in Alt-A loans (later dubbed "toxic waste"). The acquisition of these platforms, and the direct investment in real estate development projects also in the US granted record growth of its businesses, with the revenues of the capital markets unit—doing the securitization of the originated mortgage books—growing more than 55 % between 2004 and 2006. And profit also grew at record level, between 2005 and 2007, to reach an all-time highest quarterly net income of USD 4.2 Bln just few months prior to its bankruptcy!

The first cracks to the Lehman business model and solvency position appeared in the first months of 2007, when the housing market in the US started to show the potential prickle of the bubble, that eventually burst, bringing initially with it major losses on the sub and near prime mortgage exposures. Even then, Lehman's CFO was confirming that the risk for the bank was well contained and that the subprime crisis would have had little impact on the firm. Late in the year, just when its stock market price has conquered a new high, the bank started to slash 2.500 mortgage related jobs, also shutting down the BNC unit—still, the bank had clearly become one of the major players in the US mortgage market, with an overall book in excess of USD 85 Bln, and a leverage of 32 (as measured by total assets on total equity capital), and was still declaring itself as "open for business".

In March 2008, with the near collapse of Bear Stearns (the 6th largest US investment bank, forced into a last minute merger with JP Morgan), the Lehman stock price started plunging rapidly, but the bank was able to raise USD 4 Bln in the capital market. Just few months later, in June, the bank had to report a new loss for almost 3 Bln, but was still able to raise a further 6 Bln, that led to a reduction of the total leverage equal to 25 times the equity. But it was still too little and too late. As this was realized not just by the market (the stock price plunged by 77 % in the first week of September 2008) but even by the top management of the bank, the only option left on the table was, as in the case of Bearn Stern, the sale of Lehman to a more robust counterpart, no matter what the price and the governance—if still a buyer was available, notwithstanding the moral suasion of the FED.

On September 9th, the most likely option on the table vanished, as the Korean Development Bank withdrew its acquisition offer, pulling a lethal blow to the already miserable reputation of the bank—the stock price plummeted by another 45 % and the credit default swap prices on the bank's debt grew by 66 %. The failure of the negotiation was also due to the still defensive (some could have said "arrogant" behavior) of the CEO Dick Fuld. He was then also asked to leave the bank, with a new CEO appointed just days before the final bankruptcy.

On September 10th Lehman reported a new loss of USD 3.9, partially mitigated by the decrease in the market value of its debt (total write offs were approaching USD 6 Bln). After a final week end where all the remaining options were tried, notwithstanding the moral suasion of the FED (that eventually were not enough to convince Barclays to buy what was left of Lehman without any US State guarantee, and given that Bank of America was at the last minute pushed to take over Merrill Lynch, the fourth largest investment bank and also on the verge of failure) the bank had to declare its bankruptcy on September 15th, with assets in excess of USD 700 Bln.

With the hindsight of knowing how the global financial crisis unfolded, was the aggressive targeted growth at Lehman sustainable or too big of a bet? And was the shift towards the principal business one of the main culprits of the following instability of the bank? And could have the bank tried a better and more effective way of hedging or at least reducing some of its exposure towards the US real estate cycle?

And, once the crisis of the bank was becoming apparent, in the middle of 2007, what kind of last resort strategy could have helped the bank in ensuring its going concern? Should the CEO Dick Fuld being removed earlier, so as to favor a friendly sale at "no questions/no conditions attached"? And was an international Asian investor the best choice or would another major US bank being better, for Lehman and for the overall safety of the system? And, following the final decision of the FED to "let it go", what would have been the main arguments for bailing out the bank, or for letting it fail? Apart from the economic reasoning, were there political considerations? And should the aggressive and risk taking culture of Lehman being part of the equation that led to the decision?

Finally, given the final outcome of the last frantic week end, was Lehman Brothers a victim of circumstances as well—e.g. with the FED and the US Treasury willing to set an example for other banks and having to save in the very same hours Merrill Lynch (and AIG, and thus Goldman), after having already saved Bear Stearns and thinking ahead of the important contributions that was going to be requested by taxpayers, and required the approval of lawmakers, to set up and operate the TARP (Troubled Assets Relief Program) that will become the critical cornerstone to avoid the meltdown of the US banking system?

Chapter 2
Fin Tech Innovation and the Disruption of the Global Financial System

Abstract In this chapter, a more structured analysis of the wave of financial innovation—driven mainly by digitization and new technologies—but also by shadow banking players acting just outside the boundaries of regulations, is presented as it applies and impacts on the industry of financial services—with a number of potential disruptors acting across the value chain and with a different set of competitive advantages. The discussion develops therefore on the topic of the potential changes impacting across the main fundamental functions of the global financial system—from payments to lending, from investment banking to insurance and so on. A number of potential taxonomies of emerging winners are introduced and a discussion is developed on the potential strategies that could be adopted by incumbents—that could either fall victim of the innovation, or reap most of its benefits, embracing this wholeheartedly and considering also alliances with new digital players. All of this is also considered as the potential engine of the many restructuring and resolution cases that could happen because of the inability (or outright unwillingness) of some of the incumbent players to change and adapt.

2.1 The Wave of Fin Tech Innovation

Innovation is, by definition, mostly unpredictable and very often, hopefully, disruptive, as greater value creation (and migration, from incumbents unable to follow through) is usually associated with quantum leaps, and not with marginal steps. However, the current fin tech wave now unfolding in banking is really as much disruptive as it has been incremental—in the last 15 years, since the first hype related to the so called "new economy", and the subsequent burst of the DotCom financial bubble, the digital progress has been relentless even if at times subdued and low profile. The current wave of innovation, built as it is on the progressive digitization of the society and by the incremental technology now available and pushed forward by "fin tech" new players, has a number of clearly identifiable features:

C. Scardovi, *Restructuring and Innovation in Banking*,
SpringerBriefs in Finance, DOI 10.1007/978-3-319-40204-8_2

- It has become now more deliberate and targeted, often at the harm of traditional banks, as incumbents are perceived more and more as inefficient, overregulated and mostly unable to react in a prompt way. True, some of the new competitors have also been developing alliances and partnerships with traditional players, but where they see the opportunity to take them away entire businesses they increasingly do so;
- The focus of the competitive attack from digital players has become mostly associated with the greatest sources of clients' friction and pain in their relationship with existing incumbents (e.g. see the time to answer in lending, ranging from many weeks to few months for the incumbents and approaching real time for some of the new web based digital lenders, using sophisticated psychometric analysis, as well as all kind of applied analytics techniques to mine unstructured sources of data, both "formal" and "social";
- It has the greatest impact where the new digital challengers can employ business models that are platform based, data intensive and capital light, or capital less. For this competitive plays, it has become obvious how the "scarce resources" to win big is really good data and information, and smarter intelligent ways to use this information to create superior technology to serve better the clients, eventually with third party products (hence the capital light) and avoiding as much as possible any regulatory and compliance burden. As technology is mostly providing the transformation of information into intelligence, it has also become clear that long dated banks' trust (significantly tarnished after the global financial crisis and the many scandals related to misconduct—from misspelling to market rates manipulation to money laundering etc.) can be eventually replaced by the brand value of new digital players—new names and logos not even present few years ago, as it has happened in other historical industries (think at Tesla in car manufacturing);
- It has most immediate effects on very specific processes, whilst impacting significantly the global functions performed by the financial system at large—it is therefore starting in a very vertical, surgical way, to then expand horizontally, across the overall financial services value chain, to reach and get hold of the client;
- It needs to change almost continuously, as incumbents naturally try to react with similar strategies—leveraging their legacy assets, often ending up providing to the very digital challengers the infrastructure and the services they require to compete under new ways and forms—think at the payments systems and at the global infrastructure—the "plumbing"—developed by traditional players and by their consortium, and then now often managed by private equity firms and open to the new services and products of fin techs;
- It has potential implications (positive and negative—as they create new sources of capital gathering and risk diversification and transfer, but often in very opaque and less monitored ways and therefore open to frauds, cyber security issues and conduct risk) on the overall riskiness of the GFS, still not well understood, that will require new skills for the Regulators, usually slow to react and not as tech savvy as required (and sometimes not even aware of what is happening just across the traditional definition of financial services);

- It follows a development curve characterized by the continuous pressure to innovate—e.g. not a big bang event, but a chain of smaller changes driving the final disruption and with an end state that, as of now, it is really hard to predict, with a lot of uncertainty further introduced by regulatory constraints, past legacies of banks and the usual political interference (greater in financial services than in many other industries).

The important thing is however to understand how the current fin tech wave of innovation is potentially disrupting the GFS not as a Moloch per se, but as a consequence of its changing our very same style of living, from managing our job and investments, to our consumption and leisure time. Let's for example consider how the digital realm can change a consumer journey across all aspects of life—say, starting from our recurring shopping for clothes. As shown in Fig. 2.1, a number of new digital information provider are already influencing in novel ways the search and discovery part of our journey, until we almost reach the decision to buy something; then digital coupons are already driving the promotions and discounts available both on the digital and physical channels; and new digital payment options are now also allowing us to share information with our friends and with other suppliers, and the activation of digital loyalty programs will make us repeat buyers of some, and premium switchers for others … and then our feed backs and the reporting of our past transactions will be made available for future use in the

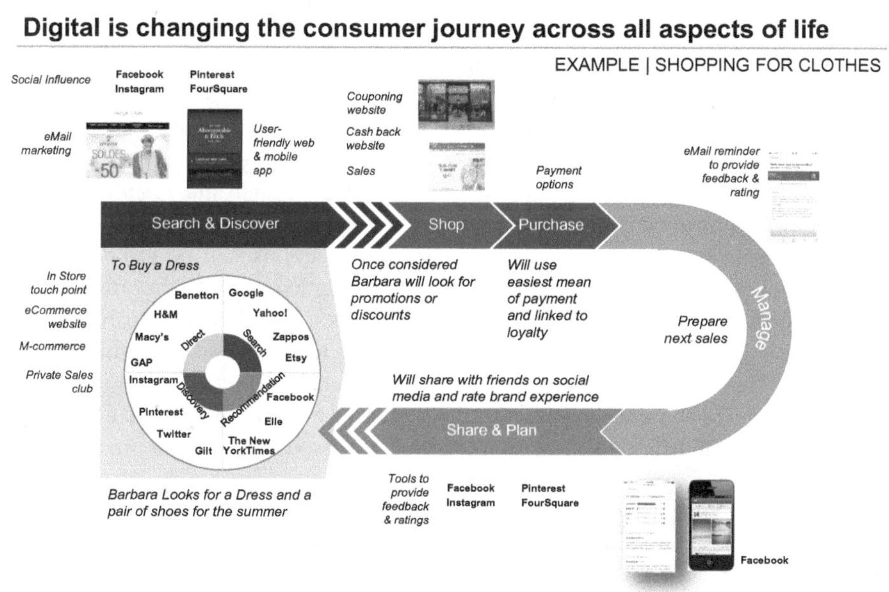

Fig. 2.1 Digital journey is changing across all aspects of life

cloud ... for us and friends and—at a cost—for other business partners acting in this ecosystem, and with the almost unavoidable digital advice on the next best product soon to follow.

A new digital journey is then exemplified as changing across all aspects of life in Fig. 2.1.

2.2 New Entrants and Disruptive Technologies

New entrants are then entering the competitive field of financial services and targeting a number of the fundamental functions traditionally performed by the likes of banks, insurance companies, asset managers, payments and credit cards companies. This promises to be a competitive war field for years to come, potentially challenging the very existence of the traditional players, often sand bagged by their non performing loans—still heritage of the last financial crisis and of the low growth environment of many developed Countries—by their quite high and rigid cost structures—nurtured and develop in the happy days when bankers were "buying money at 3 %, selling it at 6 % and playing golf from 3 p.m.", and still had a reputation, because being a banker was really good and not something almost to be excused—the last sand bag, coming from the too many scandals of the last years. The digital innovation effect, compounded by the NPLs, the high cost structure, the bad reputation... and indirectly supported by the new wave of regulation are posing the basis of the restructuring and turnaround of the banking sector to come—something that Lehman did not even had the chance to see.

In Fig. 2.2, examples of new digital players (usually also "shadow" players in their regulatory definition, as they tend to perform certain banking functions without being regulated and being short of a banking license—actually paying attention to stay away from it) are shown for the gathering and management of deposits and savings, lending, payments and settlements etc. and in the following chapters a more structured analysis across global functions will be provided. It is important to notice that the taxonomy being presented is very far from being completed and very likely to get outdated very soon, as changes are happening rapidly and with an increasing pace—lots of "fin tech" players opening up for business almost daily, with new business models and novel solutions to very old problems, such as the one of gathering and lending money—even if, sure enough one thing stand, that is that the 3–6–3 rule of old good boring banking has gone away, forever.

For the time being, and given the scope of our analysis, it is however useful to consider how these new challengers are positioning vis a vis traditional banks, and on the basis of which kind of competitive advantage:

- Most of the new challengers are in fact positioning themselves as infrastructure/service providers, therefore potentially developing, complementing or substituting tout court certain parts of the global financial "plumbing"—with economies of scale and scalability mostly attainable with shared IT platforms;

New entrants, or digital challengers, are cherry-picking profitable lines of business in financial services

Illustrative and not exhaustive

	Examples of New Non-Bank Players		Potential substitute of banks as: Producer	Distributor	Infrastructure	Main competitive advantages: Tech/ Innovation	Avoidance of regulation	Clients needs
Demand Deposits & Savings	Ally	• Online/mobile-only bank with competitive rates on checking & savings, auto loans; 900k bank customers, 4.4M auto loans	☐	☑	☐	◔	◔	◕
Lending	LendingClub OnDeck	• Online credit marketplace; over $1.6B loans ('15 Q1) • SMB loans platform; over 30k customers ('15 Q1)	☑	☑	☐	◕	◑	◕
Payment/ Settlement System	PayPal	• 10 Million payments per day, in 203 markets, 100 currencies and 157million wallets	☐	☐	☑	◕	◔	◑
Bill Pay	PayTrust	• Online, paperless bill pay	☐	☐	☑	◕	◕	◑
Merchant Processing	Square Stripe	• In-store card payments via mobile/tables; $20B trx ('14) • Online & mobile payments; worldwide in 135 currencies	☐	☐	☑	◕	◕	◕

Fig. 2.2 Digital entrants across main FS business lines

- Many others are positioning as distributors, or originators of new sales opportunities for businesses to customers, counting on a first mover's advantage to build a unique proposition and new "brand equity";
- Finally, a more limited, residual component is positioning as superior "product factory", leveraging on a specific know how ideally protected by a patent or copyright to produce some gadget better, that will then be sold by other digital distributors, or even by traditional "brick and mortar" banking players.

In Fig. 2.2—digital entrants across main financial services business lines are shown by way of examples as entering and cutting across all the main functions of the GFS, and impacting as potential producer, distributor and infrastructure provider and on the basis of different competitive advantages.

Whatever the positioning of these digital challengers along the value chain, they all share (with different weight) a number of distinctive advantages built on digital technology innovation, avoidance of regulation and a superior understanding of client needs, usually born out of their analytical capabilities used to gather, mine and interpret "big data"—structured and not, quantitative and qualitative, formal and social—coming for example from the analysis and monitoring of our reputation in the web, to discriminate on our somehow related creditworthiness; or from the information available from all kind of sources that offers new lead and lag indicators on the state of health of a business (what about monitoring, via satellite systems and the web, the occupancy of the parking lots of a supermarket during the working ours, as an indication of business flow?).

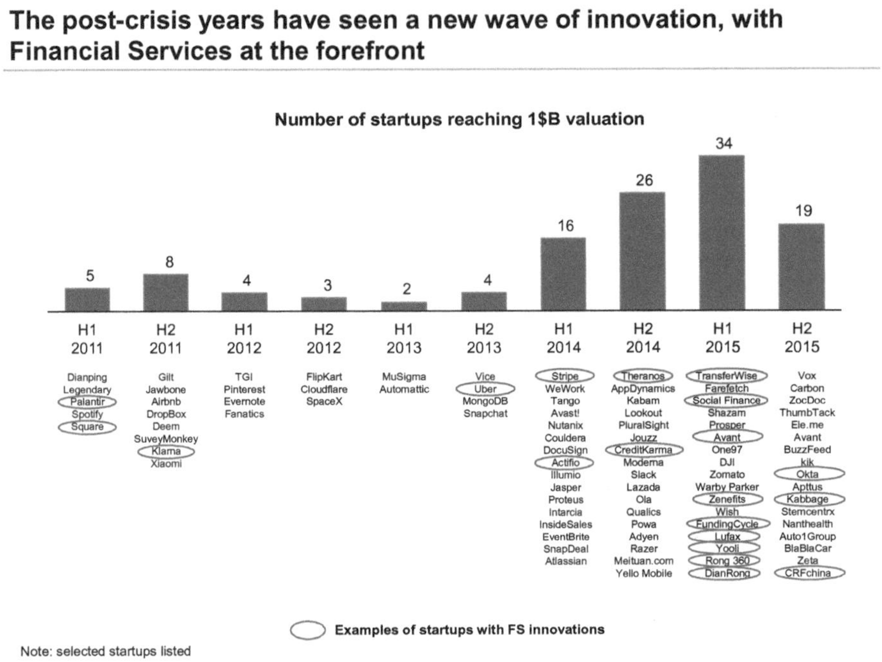

Fig. 2.3 The one billion club for start up: a fin tech business? *Source* Elaborated from CBInsight

And the returns of these digital challengers—even discounting for the hype usually surrounding any new wave of pioneers in an industry, have been in some instances impressive, with an exponentially growing number of new fin tech players reaching a 1+ USD Bln valuation (the "unicorns"), as shown in Fig. 2.3—the one billion club for start ups: a fin tech business? The figure shows all kind of start-ups across all sectors, with FS at the forefront.

This significant "digital threat" for banks—leading potentially to their restructuring, turnaround, transformation (or resolution, liquidation and demise) is compounded by the impacts coming from new, disruptive technologies getting rapidly ground at the global infrastructure level—something acting at an even larger scale and with potentially much deeper and dramatic consequences as the challenge the very "global plumbing" of the system.

Let's take for example the block chains/distributed ledgers technology (as shown conceptually in Fig. 2.4) and let's consider its potential implications over a medium-long term time horizon (5–15 years):

- Block chain technology is already being applied to a wide range of electronic payments, albeit mostly in a preliminary, testing phase (e.g. crypto currencies, with Bitcoin being the best known one) that include: payment networks for the settlement of credit card transactions; international money transfers; inter-banks settlements. There are even derivatives contracts being written in the new language, potentially allowing the running of complex derivatives on the

Disruptive technology can change banking as we know it: the example of distributed ledgers

What is a blockchain / distributed ledger architecture?

Traditional settlement network	Blockchain distributed ledger network
Transaction is guaranteed by central authority (e.g. Visa, bank)	Transaction is «witnessed» by all nodes in the network
Transaction information protected by network authority	Transaction information is semi-public: partly shared, partly cryptographed
Frauds are possible by deceiving the central authority	Reduced fraud risk due to need to "deceive" majority of nodes to settle a fraudulent transaction
The network authority requires infrastructure and resources to manage the network	A "resource light" approach is possible, with huge cost benefit in network management
Central authority maintains repository of past transactions	All transactions can be publicly linked in a "chain" up to the first one, making tampering almost impossible

Fig. 2.4 Disruptive technologies and the "block chain"

distributed ledgers technology, potentially safer, more extensively distributed (albeit in an almost anarchic way) and embedding rules of Law and conduct in its code;

- More importantly, the impact of the block-chain technology in the future could truly prove disruptive: with significant cost savings, estimated by Santander in 20 USD Bln/year for the US banking system, due to reduced back office thanks to real time, automated transaction settlement, reduced data storage needs as information is not stored behind the bank's firewalls; and reduced operational and compliance risks—because, as mentioned, the rules of Law and conduct can be written directly into the new standard code.

The potential emergence of global standards for distributed ledger settlement networks would then make a full scale, global adoption possible and welcome (a consortium with UBS, Barclays, Citi, Goldman Sachs, RBS and other major banks is already developing such a standard). Or, alternatively, bank-specific distributed ledger networks may become the norm—as anticipated in Fig. 2.4—disruptive technologies and the "block chain", forcing each bank to develop their own system (as Barclays and Santander are already doing), forcing many other out of the business covered. Or, finally, other non-banks owned distributed ledgers solutions and platforms could be developed to dominate the market and be operated and controlled by the Facebook or Google or Apple of this world, or by a new player whose name is still almost unknown.

Whatever the prevailing scenario regarding the development of digital entrants and of the new infrastructure disrupting technologies, we may reasonably expect a good number of future trends:

- Traditional banks will most likely not be able to react as quickly and effectively to the digital innovation. As global and regional banks start perceiving the real threats from disruptors, they are incapable (or less capable) to act, as their decision making and organizational set up is just ill suited for that, and as their prevailing focus is right now on implementing new regulatory requirements, and fully exiting the heavy burden of their global crisis legacies: from NPLs to decrepit IT systems to rigid cost structures. In fact, an industry—the financial services one—where regulations is mentioned a number of times as the top of mind issue of CEOs (see for example the World Economic Forum survey of global heads of strategy, 2014 and 2015) there is not great room for reaction, nor proactive planning, not to mention creative thinking;
- Regulators, on their side, may most likely not be able to see and address new risks building into the digital system that will, for sure, pop up at some point in time, as they are not trained and ready for these new rules of the game—also, the new digital realm really requires new skills and some technical prowess—not necessarily the "forte" or current regulators across the globe. Also, innovation is happening very fast, with increasing pools of talents and capital being deployed, now attracting the best talents: somebody in a garage is working to reinvent, not just steal, most of the key businesses of the GS. And, as shown by the surveys made by many MBA programs, the future employment dream of best students are not anymore investment banks, but digital start-ups and fin tech ones specifically. New risks could then be generated and go undetected and uncontrolled in the system also because of this fast paced innovation: you cannot control what is moving very fast, and cannot monitor things if they change shape continuously;
- Finally, the unprecedented pace of change and disruption could however be good news for customers, with transaction costs approaching zero and real time settlement at global level—just to mention an example applied to the payments systems. Also, they could get greater access to credit, with better transparency and even cheaper rates, with lower commission costs and a speedier response time; and they could even get equity capital and risk hedging and insurance; and cheaper, better available financial structured products. Of course, as the experience of the digital development and innovation in the other, earlier challenged industries show, a number of risks will also need to be managed by customers, including a greater risk of fraud, the cyber security of personal and privileged information and the creation of new, quasi monopolistic competitive positions able to corner the market and to almost force the customer to behave in certain ways.

2.3 Breaking up the Banking Value Chain

New digital entrants are increasingly entering the competitive field in the financial services industry and in doing so they drive the break-up of the traditionally almost fully integrated value chain. Fin tech players, in particular, are attacking valuable specific components of such value chain and with "fit-for-single-purpose" solutions. Their efficacy is then magnified, as they focus just on a single, tiny component (a service, or product), to make it much more valuable and competitive with what currently offered, and then using this single attack point to disaggregate further the original banks' service proposition and gain larger shares of it towards the end customer. A graphical representation of this is then shown in Fig. 2.5, as developed by CBinsights.

As these new fin tech players can assume different forms and shapes, it can be useful to segment them according to a two dimensional matrix, as shown in Fig. 2.6, and defined by:

- Their level of "discontinuity" brought into the financial services ecosystem (e.g. if they are just marginally improving its working, or trying to change it in a disruptive way);
- The number of "fit-for-purpose" solutions used for their entry strategy, as they may tackle single or multiple financial services functions, therefore challenging in a more or less radical way the incumbents.

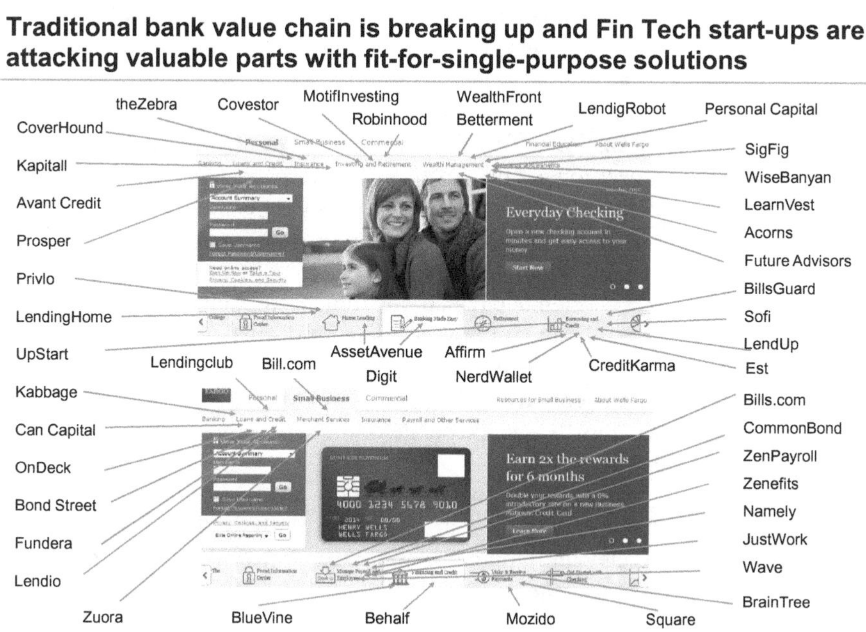

Fig. 2.5 Breaking up the banking value chain. *Source* Elaborated from CBInsight

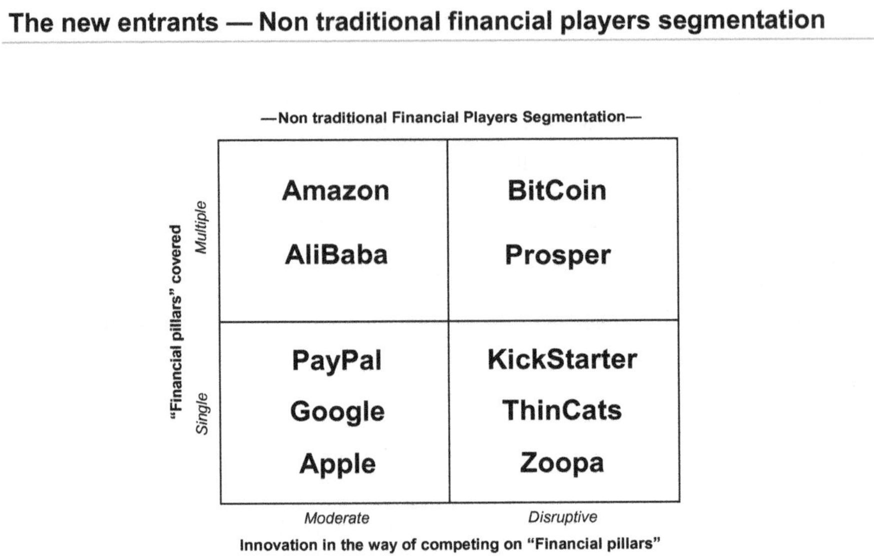

Fig. 2.6 New entrants, a dangerous lot

As identified in the figure, we could define "shedding skin" new entrants, that are trying to replace banking groups' offerings by providing incremental new services that span across newly reformulated distribution value chains (e.g. Alibaba, a search engine now offering money market funds investing primarily in the Chinese interbank market, providing interesting yield and almost instant liquidity); and "hydras", whose more disruptive value proposition tries to substitute almost completely banking players addressing some fundamental component of multiple financial services functions (e.g. Bitcoin, used as an open source online payment system, operated on a peer to peer basis, de facto working as a decentralized virtual currency); and "chameleons", that are focusing on single components of the value chain and in an incremental way—e.g. targeting "old" services with "newly improved" offers (e.g. PayPal, offering on line transactions to transfer funds electronically, and available on mobile payment instruments as well as on the web); and then, finally, "cobras" that in a more discontinuous way challenge incumbents with innovative solutions able to address pent up demand and rapidly evolving market needs (e.g. Kickstarter, a crowd funding platform for projects financed by the "backers"—individuals, mostly—in exchange of their pledges—that could either be financial or non-financial).

The segmentation proposed is shown in Fig. 2.6—new entrants, a dangerous lot.

New entrants are thus breaking up in a number of ways the different banking value chains and with relevant implications on most (if not all) of the fundamental functions of the global financial system, including:

- Payments and settlements, where electronic payments and digital currencies are now changing how consumers pay for their consumptions, and where new technologies such as the "distributed ledgers" one offers potentially a radical disruption of the system, with almost unlimited savings on cost structures;
- Funding, where new direct lending opportunities, and even equity raises opportunities via crowd funding initiatives, are now operated through digital channels and available almost real time because of the mining and analysis of a multitude of structured and unstructured data, that can now connect borrowers and savers directly, allowing a better matching of demand and supply complementary risk/return profiles;
- Asset management, where robot-advisers (based on artificial intelligence—AI—techniques and software) are now making sophisticated financial consulting on asset allocation available to almost anyone at a marginal cost approaching zero—allowing also faster responses and continuous monitoring;
- Investment banking, where frequency trading is now almost completely operated by AI systems, and new B2B platforms (e.g. dark pools, usually operated by consortia of global investment banks) allow now a direct and more efficient (if not less regulated and supervised) link between buyers and sellers;
- Insurance, where new technologies (e.g. self-driving cars, internet of things, shared economy applied to durable goods and fixed assets such as apartments and offices) are progressively revolutionizing the traditional risk underwriting, insurance and re-insurance activities, not to mention the brokerage ones.

The above mentioned five fundamental functions (or core banking areas), whilst not fully exhaustive, are at the center of the digital transformation happening right now and are worth the more detailed discussion to follow.

2.4 Innovation and Disruption in Payments

The first one to be analyzed is one of the most critical "utility" functions performed by the GFS as it allow the ordinate and timely execution of commercial trades—anything from international import-export to the most simple consumption choices done every day by consumers. Without an effective/efficient and secure payments and settlements system, we would in fact had to resort to bartering, in order to exchange things across the borders, and event to have a coffee and pastry in the morning, maybe in exchange of few fresh chicken's eggs.

A number of disrupting factors are already at play in the global payments and settlements systems, as depicted in Fig. 2.7—as new intermediaries are entering this market, and new payments rails (the infrastructure and its global "plumbing") are being developed and tested. In this new digital world, clients use these intermediaries and rails for new use cases, from NFC (near field communication) applications to MFO/CLO (merchant funded/card linked offers), and radically new technologies get tested and, if successful, increasingly adopted by both new comers

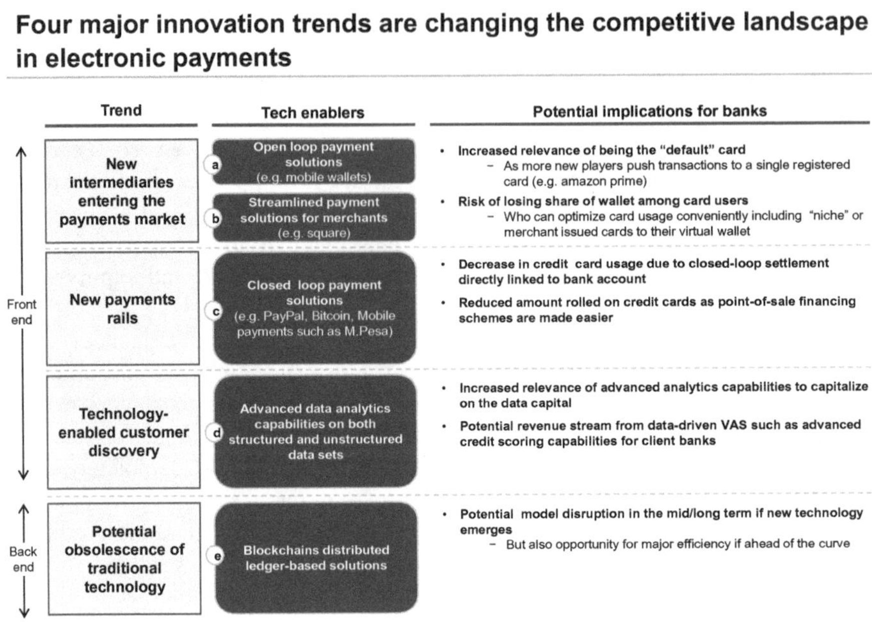

Fig. 2.7 Four main innovation trends in payments. *Source* Elaborated from World Economic Forum

and incumbents with potentially revolutionary implications. All of these dynamic factors are changing the competitive landscape in payments in a number of ways, starting from the diminishing use of cash, to the use of credit cards as stores of information, intelligence and shopping and lifestyle advice.

The summary of the four main innovation trends in payments is then represented in the following Fig. 2.7.

Starting from cash, the decrease in usage of paper and coin payments is a consolidated phenomenon in most developed Countries, where credit cards have been growing their usage for decades now. But while credit card companies and networks are still looking for ways to increase their penetration as preferred form of payment, it appears now that the general public is ready to move on from plastic and, in the name of convenience, adopt new technologies that make credit cards potentially an obsolete thing of the past, potentially leading to their disappearance, in favor of other digital means (starting from smartphones, which can already embed crypto keys that allow for fast, NCF based, payments—with connected reporting, information storage and exchanges).

New solutions are then becoming available. Most of them have as an end game the streamlining of the payment process for consumers and merchants, both in-store and online—less of a bother, quicker and more transparent and information reach, and even more secure. Both are likely to impact and disrupt in a major way the competitive environment, and the working and the economics of this fundamental function played by the global financial system and by its traditional banking players—already harmed by the significant shrinkage of the inter-banking commissions. One of the earliest examples was Amazon's 1-click payment option where, after a client have chosen a default credit card, all following purchases can be processed on that same card, without further input needed and with one simple click. Uber's payments are today already processed in the same way.

Examples of similar "open loop" payment solutions that leverage existing payment networks and improve the user experience are also available for in-store purchases and offered in connection with digital wallets as already offered by the likes of Android Pay, Apple Pay or Samsung Pay (with few incumbents trying to catch up). The threat that these payment methods constitute to traditional credit cards players is twofold:

- They intermediate the buyer and the payment provider, who loses its direct relationship with the final end user. In this way, all the card's additional services, benefits and marketing offers become more complicated to communicate for the card issuer and some of their value gest intermediated by others. The new payment intermediary (i.e. the provider of the digital wallet) has instead an easy and direct access to the consumer and can offer its own "value added services" (e.g. reporting) to grow and consolidate the relationship;
- The new system increases the relevance of being the default card, creating a "winner takes it all" environment—the master card will connect to a number of slave cards, but will clearly control most of the flows and manage the direct relationship and ownership of the final customer. This reduces the impact of differentiation factors such as card design or brand and can marginalize niche or merchant-issued cards.

In addition to the above mentioned "open loop" payment systems that rely on existing networks, new "closed loop" payment solutions are also gaining traction in everyday purchases, but are obviously more controlled. More specifically, the closed loop solutions integrate in a single entity the acquirer and the payment network.

Both open loops and closed loops payments solutions (and the streamlined payments solutions available for merchants) are aiming at improving the overall experience and usability for both customers and merchants and have major impacts front-to-back, e.g. from the front-end customer part of the value chain to the back office part—as shown in Fig. 2.8—open and closed loop innovation in payments.

The best known example of closed loop system is PayPal that allows the use of funds from a "PayPal account" to make payments both online and in-store through the PayPal digital wallet. Closed loop solutions potentially eliminate credit cards networks from the payments equation—even though most of them allow consumers to fund transactions via the traditional payment network ecosystem too. In theory, and in practice as well, in the case of PayPal, these new closed loop systems can follow the entire customer journey, progressively leveraging different capabilities (built or bought, as PayPal did over time to extend aggressively along the most

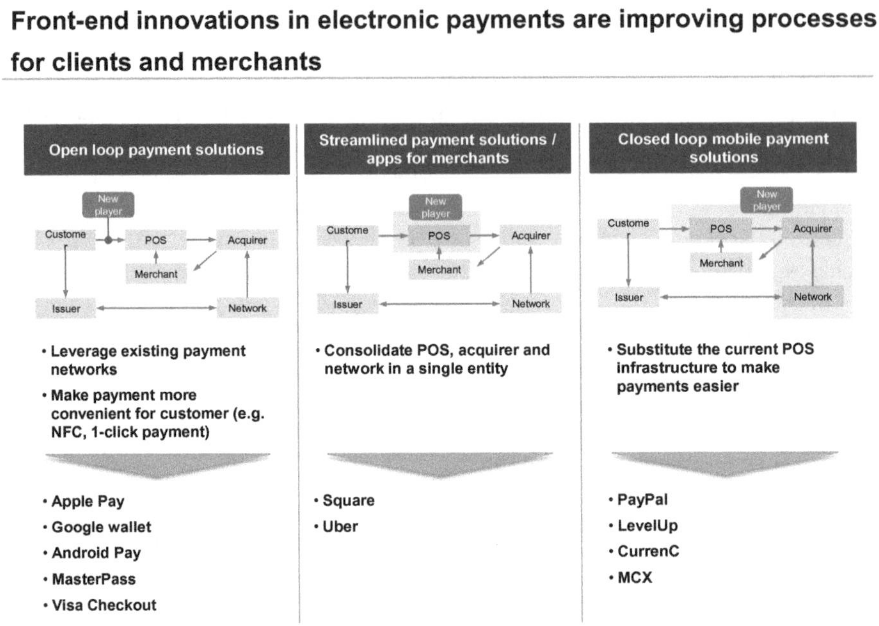

Fig. 2.8 Open and closed loop innovation in payments. *Source* Elaborated from World Economic Forum

juicy part of the value chain) to get hold of the client and of most of the value adding phases of his shopping journey—as shown graphically in Fig. 2.9—PayPal investment strategy: following the consumer journey.

The new intermediaries in payments may then be adopting different models and have the backing from a very heterogeneous range of mixed hardware-software (Samsung, Apple), software (Google) or e-commerce (Ebay/PayPal) companies, and have one critical element in common: their data applied analytics capabilities.

On one side, digital wallet services launched by new digital players, can aggregate different payment methodologies, such as cards from different issuers and payments linked to e-banking platforms, and as such they can gather more information on consumers' behavior than any of the individual traditional payment providers. Thanks to world-class big data management capabilities, new payment players can then take a data-driven approach to understanding customers and businesses and are eager to use this information to offer new services and grab market share from other, often non related business (acting as brokers, they can gain a share of the revenue pools of other business as intermediation/origination fee).

On the other side, traditional financial institutions (or "incumbents") can also benefit from the rise of digital payments that, albeit intermediated, increase the data availability and richness compared to cash transaction. So far the main applications of payment data analysis were on marketing and advertising, but it is easy to see how an increased visibility into individuals' and businesses' cash flow and

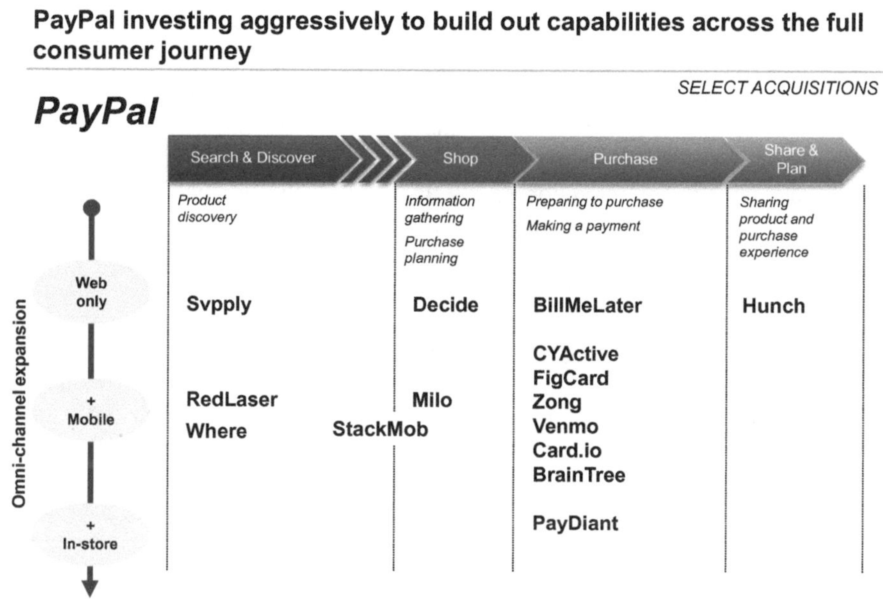

Fig. 2.9 PayPal investment strategy: following the consumer journey

spending patterns will improve the data owner's ability to extend loans to customers previously less understood and therefore underserved.

Switching the focus of our discussion from new digital players to traditional financial institution, there may be three main consequences for banks from the ongoing transformation in the world of payments:

- They may be losing control over their customers experience and therefore ultimate fidelization. Incumbents may therefore end up losing some or most of their control over their customers' transaction experience as digital wallets consolidate digital payment platforms and keep adding high value added services;
- They may however react by develop more accurate customer targeting to "defend their turf". Leveraging data—that banks has in excess, also from past history—on specific customer segments will become an essential component of any commercial strategy to gain a dominant share of the digital wallet of the targets clients and to encourage or drive more frequent usage of specific payment means in a competitive market;
- They may also counterattack by developing a stronger and more prominent relationship with merchants. Incumbents' ability to partner with merchants will become a critical component of their strategies to drive merchant-specific usage, enabling merchant-issued credit cards, or becoming a preferred partner for cards and payments on their platforms and offering them MFO-CLO (merchant/card linked offers) services.

2.5 The Distributed Ledger Technology and Challenge

Credit cards are not the only payment product being threatened by new technologies anyway. The rise of the "Bitcoin" and of other cyber-securities and of other cryptography-based forms of payments (the so-called crypto-currencies) has now focused the incumbents' attention on the technology that is enabling it, e.g. the distributed ledgers one, whose potential applications are much more relevant and extensive than the crypto currencies themselves, and is now getting the attention (and the invested money) of both venture capital funds and banks.

A "distributed ledger" technology is based on a system that, following a very basic interpretation, is a record of data that allows verifying and certifying who is the final and definitive owner of a certain value, or asset. Unlike other traditional payment schemes, distributed ledgers do not have a central administrator or a central data storage—e.g. they are born as distributed and, in a way "anarchic" as they are ruled by the web following rules that are kind of an unmanaged democracy (if most of the participants believe this asset is your, your it is).

The "ledger" is then distributed because it is de facto replicated among many different nodes in a peer-to-peer network, and a consensus algorithm ensures that each node's copy of the ledger is identical to every other node's copy. The recognition of the owners of assets happens thanks to a cryptographic signature that is apparently really difficult to break. Besides, all new operations are linked to previous events in an uninterrupted chain that is then reproduced in each copy of the ledger. In this way, it is virtually impossible to tamper with the rightful ownership of an asset, as one would need to alter the ledger in all (or at least the majority) of its instances, that are, as we said, distributed across the network and are therefore difficult to break or pollute and manipulate.

The advantages that such a technology offers are significant: first of all, it allows for a very "infrastructure light" system, as the network is based on a peer-to-peer architecture. Then, it is applicable easily in contexts where traditional networks are more complicated to manage, such as in the case of international payments systems—where there isn't a single central institution overseeing the market. And finally, it is more reliable and less easy to deceive and break compared to a traditional centralized network management scheme.

It all then promises to bring a true revolution in payments, as shown in Fig. 2.10.

Distributed ledgers are not however immune to shortcomings: while individual transactions are safer, they are also more subject to large scale hacking, and the anonymity of accounts makes approved transfers irreversible. Besides, the value of cryptocurrencies is not linked to any underlying instrument or to the credibility of a central institution (that's why we have referred the system as "anarchic" or as "unmanaged democracy"), and as a result they tend to have a much higher volatility compared to traditional currencies, and being less transparent, publicly monitored and regulated (if at all). It follows therefore that they are more at risk of being used as a mean for illicit business (they have been named overtime as the currency for drug dealers). Bitcoin is the best known cryptocurrency and the most widely

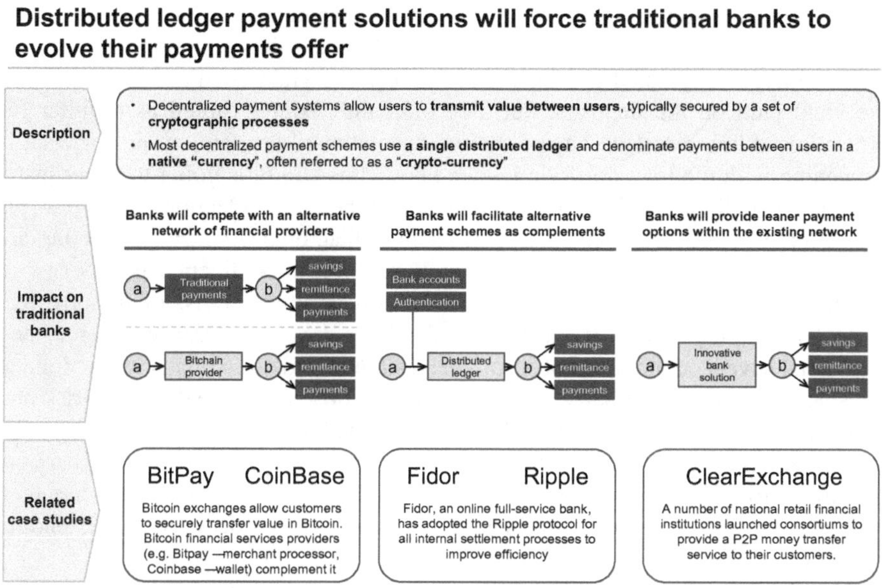

Fig. 2.10 Distributed ledgers, a new revolution in payments. *Source* Elaborated from World Economic Forum

accepted, but there is a large number of such crypto-currency being created by the day, including for instance Ripple and LiteCoin, both built for very low cost instant exchanges of value.

Whilst at the moment the practical applications of distributed ledgers, other than for minting crypto-currencies, are modest, the incumbent banks themselves are investing heavily to create the future reference system for shared, distributed ledgers technology, with the purpose to drive costs down and potentially reduce their operational (regulatory, conduct, fraud etc.) risks. The main areas of applications would then be the payment networks for the settlement of credit cards transactions, the international money transfers, the inter-bank settlements, the syndicated lending settlement but potentially, all kind of financial instruments, spot or forward.

2.6 Innovation and Disruption in Lending

Among the consequence of the sub-prime mortgages crisis of 2008 and of the subsequent credit crunch, there was the exposure of one of the limitations of the traditional lending model: the imperfect matching of savers and borrowers from a risk appetite standpoint (not to mention their duration mismatch). Traditional intermediaries hold savings from a wide range of retail, corporate and institutional clients, who receive a remuneration that reflects the level of risk of the intermediary itself. Using the funds received, intermediaries originate loans to extend to borrowers and earn interest to remunerate the credit risk—thus profiting from the net interest margin originated by the spread between the yield obtain on the loans and the yield paid on the deposits, but they offer they equity capital as a buffer (or protection of first resort) to ensure the savings gathered are safe, no matter what is happening with the loan portfolio (as we know, this equity is going to cover just a fraction—usually a 3–6 %—of this savings, and then the protection of last resort is then offered by the insurance protection schemes that, on a Country basis so far, are protecting the clients' savings up to circa Euro 100k in continental Europe).

This is a traditional "pool" model, where all savers share the risk of all borrowers (net of the equity buffer of the bank and of the deposit insurance scheme) and individual savers cannot control who receives their funds—as this is really done at the sole discretion of the bank. Savers can then choose the desired level of risk and return by giving their funds to a different intermediary, but it is in most cases a loose matching. After the crisis, this has had the effect of excluding higher risk borrowers form the lending market, as no major financial intermediary has then been dealing with these segments. The net effect has been a decrease of the lending available.

This lending gap was fertile ground for the rise of alternative lending platform, based on a "peer to peer" (P2P) model—essentially a radically different business model, as depicted in Fig. 2.11, where alternative lending platforms match directly the lending needs of borrowers with willing lenders, and the contractual obligations

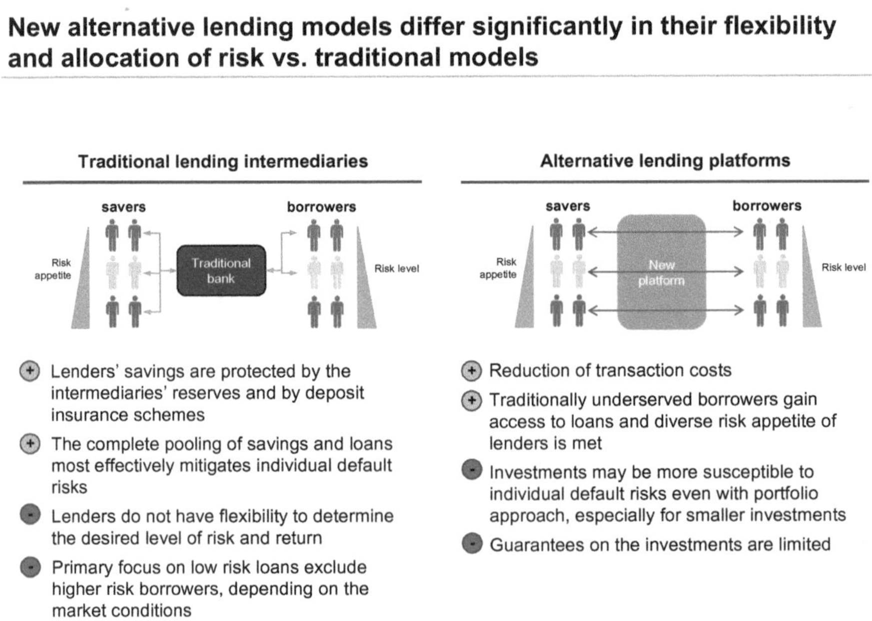

Fig. 2.11 New P2P lending models. *Source* Elaborated from World Economic Forum

exist directly between the borrowers and the lenders as the platform provide just mere intermediation services (on top, they can offer risk analysis and related advisory services, as reporting and asset allocation planning and monitoring, but the risk underwriting remains at sole discretion of the lenders). As a consequence, their profit and loss model is also different, as it is not based on a net interest rate margin (or spread), but on originating commissions for the match making, and further ones for the risk advisory component.

The main taxonomies of P2P new lending models is then represented in Fig. 2.11.

These new platforms started emerging both in Europe and in the US and quickly overcame their initial focus on less served markets like the subprime one, and started offering a broader value proposition, with better client service and improved funds adjudication processes compared to traditional lenders. For instance, Zoopa, one of the first P2P lenders to emerge, today targets only prime lenders with a seamless, very quick to answer, origination process and very low interest rates, made possible by a world class loan adjudication model.

Another relevant example is Amplify Capital, a startup with focus on data applied analytics that offers small unsecured loans to micro and small firms, leveraging merchant acquiring data for adjudication. This information is an accurate indication of a company's cash flow, is readily accessible and helps to calculate micro daily instalments for loan repayment. The company does not only try to disintermediate current lenders, but also offers the same service to third party banks, thus driving change within traditional intermediaries. Other models, such as the Lending Club, are instead just complementing the traditional intermediaries lending offering, as in the case of its partnership with Union Bank to address its subprime borrowing needs.

2.7 Innovation and Disruption in Asset Management

The consequences of the financial crisis have been far-reaching for the asset gathering and investment management industry as well. Few asset classes all but disappeared, and some large institutions went out of business, with regulations becoming significantly tighter. However, another often overlooked effect may be the one with the deepest impact on money management for the years to come: private investors, and in particular younger individuals, either "professionals" and "non-professionals", who experienced two significant recessions over the last 15 years, have growth to be wary of active, alpha seeking (but high commissions charged) investment strategy and in particular of the investment managers themselves.

The old mantra of "beating the market" does not attract younger investors (in particular Millennials) any more; not at least not as much as "balanced portfolio" and "market-following, low-fee" beta tracking investment strategies—not to mention long term institutional, that have started to compare the absolute returns—net of fees—generated by hedge funds and private equity firms—with the ones easily gotten by replicating the market.

This newly developed investor preference has found a perfect match in the Fin-Tech innovations being introduced in asset management, first and foremost automated investment management advisory platforms (the so called "robo-advisors"). These platforms are pairing the reliability and consistency of data-driven, automated investment decisions with a lower cost-to-serve per client—with marginal costs potentially approaching zero, once the technology has been built and is running above a certain minimal scale threshold. While robo-advisors today still manage a small share of world's wealth, their rise to prominence has been much quicker than initially expected: in 2014, the most optimistic forecasts projected USD 250 Bln of AUM circa by 2020, while today that figure seems to be fairly reachable by the end of 2016, with more than USD 2 Tnl projected for 2020.[1]

Another threat for asset managers, besides automation and passive trading strategies, is the increasing empowerment of private investors, who have access to an unprecedented amount of market information, often coming from social sources, and can perform trades independently from other financial intermediaries and through convenient, full service online trading solutions. Private investors are more and more looking for opinions and insights from their peers for what has been called "social trading", and are crowd-sourcing investing ideas as well, often in newly dedicated platforms such as Estimize, Covestor or StockTwits.

Luckily enough, not all Fin-Tech innovations seem to work against traditional asset and investment management firms: from a technological standpoint, for asset managers it has actually never been easier or cheaper to deliver state-of-the-art services to wealth management clients, thanks to a number of digital startups that specialize in small parts of the investing value chain, making them cheaper and more efficient. As a matter of example:

- In data collection and analysis, firms such as Novus and Kensho make it easy to consolidate data from a number of sources, also for regulatory purposes, and they allow to analyze different investment scenarios with real-time performance projections, at affordable prices and without any investment required;
- In trade strategy and execution, managers can analyze large amounts of public data collected by firms such as Ayasdi, to develop independently their own analysis and draw out correlations and outlayers;
- For transaction monitoring and risk management, RedKite offers an intelligent algorithm that detects transactions not compliant with internal policies, thus allowing lower costs of risks at low operating costs;
- Finally, for regulatory and compliance, a number of new players such as FundApps make it easy to manage disclosures to shareholders of supervisory entities with automated, cloud-based services.

[1] AT Kerneay, 2015.

Speaking more broadly, external market trends are also pushing global and regional asset managers towards a more radical business transformation, with an active role played by digital innovation:

- The competition for wealthy clients could be further supported and increased by the availability of cheaper and faster online tools and automated services—potentially offering the opportunity to deliver really good services ("value for money") to affluent and mass market clients as well;
- The commoditization of the services being offered is also promoted by the automated investment management platforms that are able to standardize traditionally highly personalized, value added services at a fraction of costs, given their embedded digital innovation;
- Finally, the higher financial literacy of the client base is further spurred by the availability of easy to use digital data analytics tools, for getting information, elaborating investment intelligence and executing structured investment strategies and asset allocations.

2.8 Innovation and Disruption in Investment Banking

Much like in asset management, recent innovations in global investment banking have also taken a twofold direction, being guided either by the new "social" side of doing business, or by the availability of new disruptive technologies. Starting from the latter, in the global wholesale markets we have recently observed the emergence of a number of new platforms able to connect multiple intermediaries of buyers and sellers to facilitate the discovery of counterparts and realize therefore a better match making and overall market liquidity. The new platforms can cover most of the products spectrum, from fixed income, currency and commodities, to equity-like products and both spot and forward positions, for primary and secondary markets, as shown below—see Fig. 2.12—new platforms connecting multi-intermediaries.

Whilst traditional capital raising intermediaries have been traditionally directly structuring products for their customers, emerging, alternative platforms can now act as marketplaces—playing de facto as facilitators and providing an easy to use "discovery process" to close the deals—where contractual obligations exists directly between individual investors and investments opportunities (with usually no role at all for financial intermediaries and with no "clearing house" role played by the company managing the web-based digital market, as it does not act as counterpart of the deal). These new platforms can then act by disintermediating the main financial intermediaries, as shown in Fig. 2.13.

Going back to the former element, the new "social" side of the business, the most relevant among recent applications of "capitalism for everybody" principle to investment banking is probably the crowdfunding phenomenon, where alternative

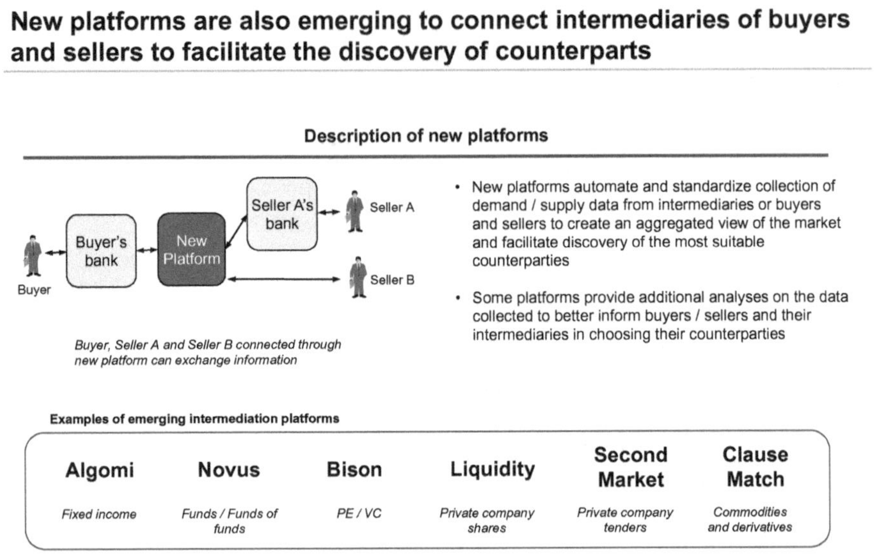

Fig. 2.12 New platforms connecting multi-intermediaries. *Source* Elaborated from World Economic Forum

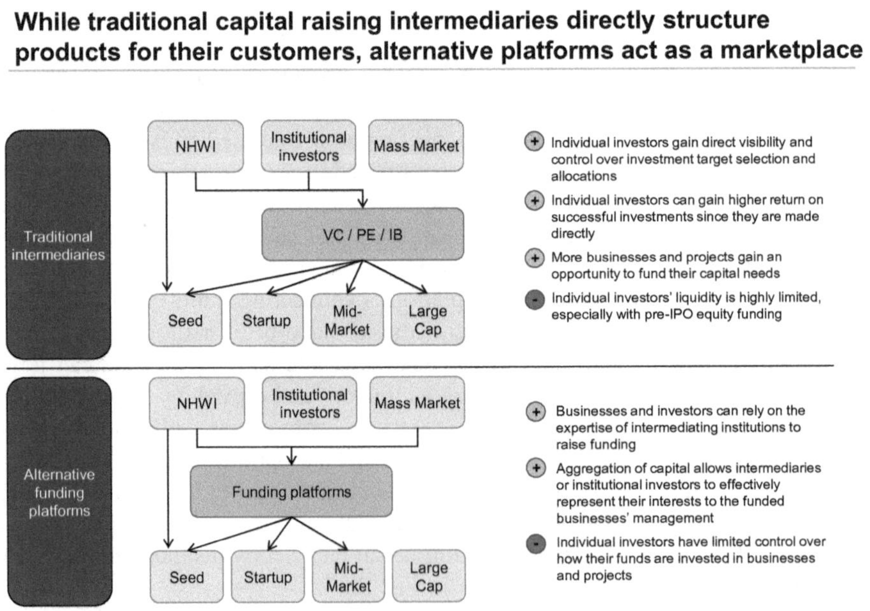

Fig. 2.13 New platforms disintermediating financial intermediaries. *Source* Elaborated from World Economic Forum

funding platforms offer a "match-making" service for investors to discover businesses and projects, relying on the "wisdom of the crowd" or of other more seasoned investors. In these crowd-funding platforms, private investors contract directly with the owner/entrepreneur/promoter of the investment opportunity—based on its related business plan, without the structuring, origination and distribution services provided by investment banks.

Dedicated crowdfunding platforms cover then the whole spectrum of investing purposes, from seed-stage funding (Seedr), to social/"capitalism for everybody" investing—offering relatively low risk/return profiles (Abundance), to low-cost capital increases for larger companies (CrowdCube).

Finally, on the technological end of innovation we can also find automated trading. Algorithm-driven trading itself is not new: it became popular in the 90s, and it has been focused for a long time on identifying and exploiting arbitrage opportunities by leveraging the "delays" in market adjustments. Algorithmic trading has been hugely profitable for many years already, but it appears to have peaked around the turn of the decade, and is today decreasing in utilization and profitability—also driven by the collapsing costs of hyper fast connections and transactions. The TABB group estimates that total revenues of high frequency trades decreased from 7.2 Bnl USD in 2009 to 1.3 Bln USD in 2014. Recent technological development could then become the trigger for a second wave of automated trading strategies, more complex and sophisticated than the first one. Automated, event-driven trading for instance is becoming a reality thanks to firms like SemLab and SNTMNT. They have developed technologies able to analyze news, social media and internet traffic in real time and identify autonomously events capable of influencing the stock price and thus offer stock pick advice.

The focus of automated trading can thus move from the mere offering of market information only (i.e. movements in the price of securities) to real-life events risk analysis to investment advice. New trading algorithms will then most probably benefit from larger data sets and deeper analytics capabilities, and they will allow the discovery and utilization of new, unexpected factors relevant to securities performance. The data analytics market is therefore getting more and more crowded, and both large incumbents (SAS, IBM) and upcoming startups (Palantir, Ayasdi) are working to offer access to "big data" aggregation from a large number of sources, and remote analysis capabilities.

As a conclusion, it is worthwhile to note that so far automated trading almost entirely relied on the human factor as far as the trading strategy was concerned. Machines were the fastest and most powerful executors of a strategy decided by market experts with business, economics and mathematics degrees. Today, there is a large number of startups that are working to change this, introducing self-learning and self-adapting "machine intelligence" (or "leaning machines") capable to ask questions, test hypotheses, come up with the most profitable trading strategy and adapt it when markets change, all without human intervention. Examples of firms working on this field are Sentient, Rebellior Research and Ayasdi.

2.9 Innovation and Disruption in Insurance

In insurance, a large number of forces is putting pressure on incumbents at all stages of the value chain—from reinsurance/insurance production to distribution to post sales, as graphically shown in the following Fig. 2.14—disrupting the insurance value chain.

Starting from the origination and distribution of insurance policies (both life and P&C), online aggregators that allow customers to compare prices and purchase insurance products directly online are already gaining significant traction and may be displacing in the short run traditional distribution channels as customer preferences change (getting more and more price sensitive and seeking the transparency that will allow them to get a better deal—an insurance product is something you need to have, not that you want to have, and products are sold, not bought) and insurance products gest more and more commoditized and thus comparable.

What's more, large tech firms showed interest in joining this market—it is often commented as the one, within financial services, that is going to be easily disrupted and challenged by digital innovators. For instance, Google acquired Beat ThatQuote, a UK e-aggregator, charging insurers up to $54 per click. Examples of other insurance aggregators are Gocompare, Money supermarket, and BizInsure (for businesses), with many more popping up by the day. As a reference point,

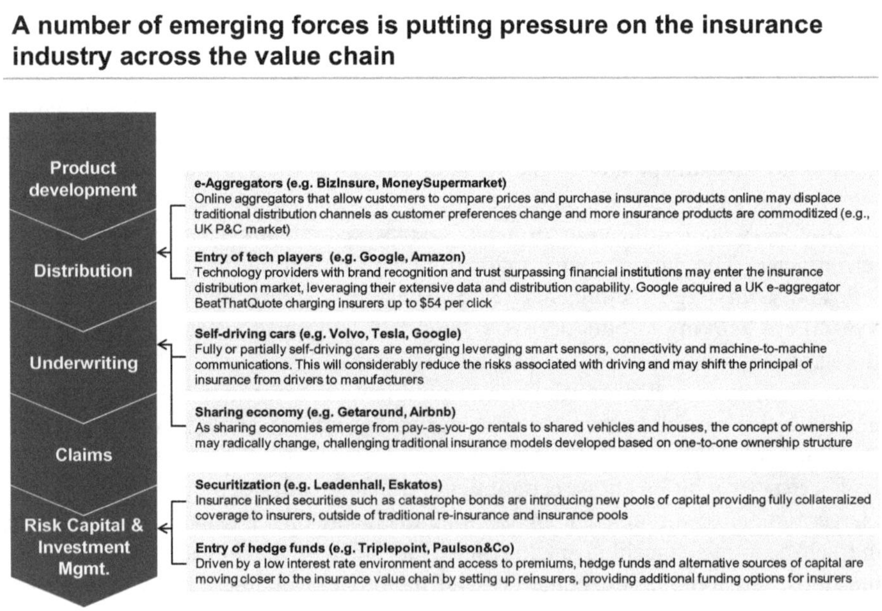

Fig. 2.14 Disrupting the insurance value chain. *Source* Elaborated from World Economic Forum

Alibaba (a Chinese version of Ebay, born out of the eCommerce opportunity) has become by far the main distributor of insurance policies in mainland China, with a dominant market share versus traditional insurance and banking incumbents, and it is becoming supervised by the relevant regulators as it could pose systemic risks of its own, should something go wrong in its (albeit indirect) risk underwriting.

In insurance underwriting, it is then the underlying market that is changing at a fast pace: as the "internet of things" is already spreading at large scale, with a number of products being connected over the web and sharing continuously information and data, and as sharing economies emerge from pay-as-you-go rentals to shared vehicles and houses, the very concepts of real time risk monitoring and of property's ownership may end up radically changing, challenging traditional insurance models developed based on one-to-one ownership structure.

In the coming years, self-driving cars may further revolutionize the insurance market, reducing the risks associated with driving and shifting the principal risk of insurance from drivers to manufacturers (Volvo has already announced that it will take responsibility of damages caused by its future self-driving cars). All this will create more standardized and commoditized and thus "transparent" risks, thus putting further pressure on insurers' margins. As the disruptive forces here are coming from outside the insurance world, we should also mention the increasing role of "shadow insurance underwriting", similarly to what we said for shadow banking—as risks are shifted very quickly across the system, they tend to end up being owned by non-regulated, or less regulated entities, thus increasing the risks of misconduct, fraud, embezzlement and mismanagement.

In the management of risks and investments, insurance linked securities are then introducing new pools of capital for insurers, providing fully collateralized coverage, outside of traditional re-insurance and insurance pools. Leaders in this market are financial firms such as Leadenhall and Eskatos. At the same time, as insurers are divesting from hedge funds (also because of the new, higher regulatory capital requirements), hedge funds are setting up reinsurers, further increasing their funding and risk transfer options. Examples of funds that entered the reinsurance industry are Triplepoint and Paulson & Co., with many more following this trend.

Viewed from a more high level perspective, we can identify three trends as having a potentially significant long term impact—we can also see them as answers to the emerging forces in the global insurance business:

- The consolidation of the market by mega insurers will bring about new economies of scale and scope. But it could also prove a short lived competitive reply to the disruptive forces of innovation. No consolidation play can in fact stop short the new business models now revolutionizing the market that can actually mimic and replicate the M&A game in a virtual way, e.g. pooling together multiple resources through a web based system, linking in a more efficient and effective way insurance holders and providers;
- The rise of multi-line policies could also address few adverse selection and moral hazard problems, whilst offering further economies of scale and scope and

helping in the diversification of the risks being underwritten, by spreading them out to an even broader and more international market of final holders. However, the aggregation offered by incumbent multi-line insurers can be easily replicated by new digital players, again leveraging their virtual presence on the web and their ability to pool together multiple actors and in a fairly efficient and effective way—in a virtually real time, borderless way;

- Finally, the shifting focus to niche markets and commercial lines is also a rational answer to the threats posed by digital players, as it allows the further efficiencies that can be gained by focalization and increased dominance in a specific business line. However this strategy is also fairly replicable by digital players, which are actually less encumbered by multiple layered legacy systems and therefore can afford to invest in few things and with a state of the art technological solution. In all these cases, we see how the "logical reaction" is then followed and copied by "smart digital competitors" that keep getting new ground and promising to further disrupt the insurance industry, for their shareholders but also their clients' benefit.

The secular trends impacting the insurance market are then summarized in Fig. 2.15.

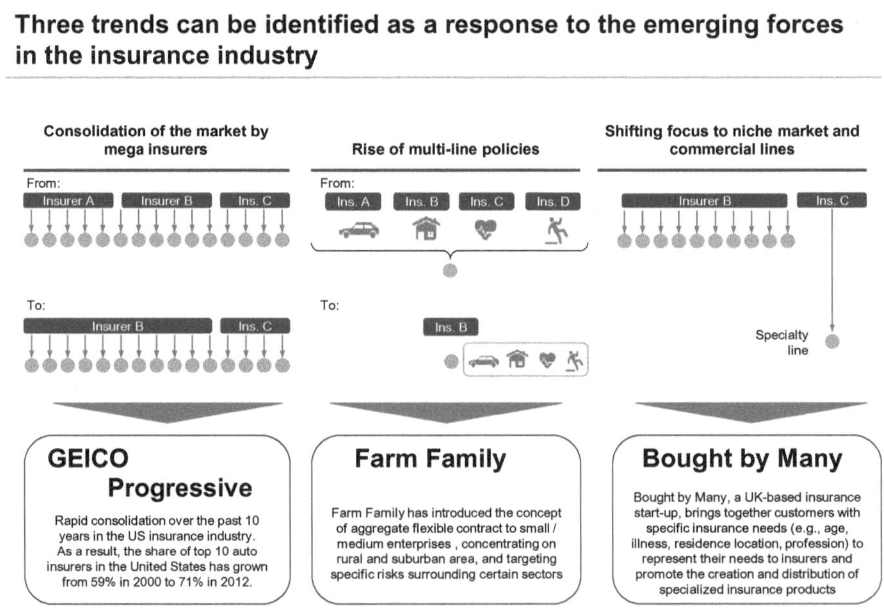

Fig. 2.15 Secular trends impacting the insurance market. *Source* Elaborated from World Economic Forum

2.10 Transform or Die (The Quick and the Dead)

Despite a number of big headlines and high resounding announcements, with investments for hundreds of millions announced, most of the incumbent "traditional" banks are still at their infancy stage of the journey to digitization—or are just planning a faulted one that is likely to cause them even more pain and financial losses. As we have argued that the digital transformation theme will be more and more crucial for the financial services industry, and we have also suggested how a new and more long lasting, structural wave of banks bankruptcies could be fostered by the emergence of the new digital disruptors, it almost logical to wander why global and regional banks, with their still big pockets, recognized brand and sizable business have been so far so incapable to react in a proper and effective way—this should be top of their CEO's agenda after all!

Still incapable they have proved to be so far, and for a number of reasons, including significant organizational and technological constraints and, most importantly, cultural issues that drive in turn the unwillingness to change on the side of some of the key, historical constituencies of the bank (as any change entails some power struggle and many losers). As this is going to impact on the likelihood of the banking organizations to transform and survive in the evolving competitive markets, it becomes more and more important to understand what blocks them to change and consider the most reasonable options to overcome these constraints:

- Most of the new digital applications and systems are built anew by digital players, whilst have to be built on existing legacy systems ("spaghetti wrangles") on the side of the incumbents, with higher costs and complexity (as there are also many legacies, not usually well interconnected) and execution risks, and typically with a less compelling end-game (in the best scenario, they will likely end up cannibalizing most of the existing business of the "brick and mortar" bank). The obvious solution would be to consider a full legacy system overhaul—but that is going to be a very complex, costly and lengthy exercise for the ones who dare. Or the development, in a more lean and less capital intensive way, of the new digital services as completely outside the boundaries and the systems and even the physical premises of the "old bank", with the risk of inconsistencies, regulatory constraints and multiple checks to be cleared, but with the flexibility of an easier spin off/carve out, should the competitive strategy suggest this is the best way to go;
- Many branches are already under-utilized and therefore the further development of new digital channels would imply that the migration of clients to the new channels is just making more of them redundant (as long as the people working in them). Despite a drastic network reduction and several attempts to re-invent the "branch of the future", the scope and magnitude of the change required is still something strongly resisted internally—with big transition and redundancy costs making things even more difficult. The most effective solution would then need to address governance and organizational issues, and find a proper balance with the branches as help desks/advisory points—without forgetting that

everything at the end is done by people and that culture is playing a big role—as intangible and difficult to change it always is;

- Many skills and roles today still present in banking are also likely to be "traditional" in nature and content, and with significant gaps versus the skills and competencies that would be required to run a truly new digital offering—and these gaps in the competencies could prove even harder to address, particularly if the change required needs to be operated inside-out, with internally lead innovation processes that revolutionize the way the bank engages with customers front to back. An HR policy based on aggressive targets of external hires would contribute in overcoming these gaps, whilst on the other end introducing a number of other risks—and requiring the bank's capability to attract, integrate and retain the new key employees.

Notwithstanding these many difficulties, incumbent financial institutions—if able to address these shortcomings in the most effective way—have still ample opportunities and financial and commercial resources to try and defend old business, and capture new ones, and grow revenues coming from the digital transformation challenge, with a number of potential roles to be played along the journey:

- As participants, they could actively utilize third-party services to enhance their current businesses via digital capabilities. As an example, they could start distributing merchant funded offers to progressively substitute their internally managed, bank funded loyalty program and develop an adjacent business (as a digital to store match maker, helping buyers in their buying choices and merchants in their sales effort);
- As business builders, they could actively invest in digital capabilities as a core competence and in other critical assets to expand beyond their current businesses. As an example, they could build smart data applied analytics capabilities, able to analyze data and create new intelligence, to grow new businesses in the information services area and sell them to SME/corporate clients;
- As market creator/makers, they could build entirely new businesses by pursuing new market opportunities created or just potentially supported by digital transformation—e.g. re-inventing brick and mortar payments systems and then building integrated offerings around them.

From and execution perspective, the transformation of the banks' operating model—as required to pursue these more and more ambitious goals and improve their productivity, but also to reinvent in novel ways their business model—would also entail different steps, in a potentially sequential way:

- As practitioners, banks could start actively utilizing digital capabilities to streamline their internal processes to capture cost savings—e.g. using digital signatures would allow them to reduce transaction costs and reduce the service time to client; or using remote deposit capture would help them in offering to clients a new value added service—improving their overall customer experience;

Several opportunities to enhance the operating model: key to assess the current level and set the ambition

Opportunity Areas	Practitioner	Advanced	Best-in-Class
Transforming Customer Interfaces and Processes *End-to-End Customer Experience*	Simplify and improve customer/user interfaces Reduce branch footprint	Develop new mechanisms and tools for customer engagement (e.g., in-app messages, automation)	Adopt digital as the primary means for interacting with customers that enhances satisfaction & loyalty Spin-off/outsource non-critical manual processes
Realigning and Integrating Critical Decision-Making Engines *Internal Processes*	Straight-thru processing of key data — eliminating manual processing	Handling of complex algorithms efficiently and consistently	Access to real-time targeted information (data) in an easy-to-use format/interface
Re-Architecting Databases and Applications *Enterprise Architecture*	Eliminate redundant and desolate infrastructure Rationalize vendors and suppliers Active information management to reduce data stored	Consistent application stack with common integration layer — reducing maintenance, speeding new development, driving innovation Rationalize applications, possibly outsource some	Integrated data management — integrated customer master, consistent data structures across brands, service lines, and channels Co-opetition — joint platforms with competitors for non-competitive processes

Fig. 2.16 Moving targets along the road to banks' digitization

- As advanced, banks would invest in digital platforms to introduce new tools and eliminate costly, redundant processes. As an example, in-app messages could replace traditional customer communications tools and allow new forms of consumption by collaboration; or new digital platforms for payroll and benefits could change the way the company interacts and communicates with its own employees;
- As best in class, banks would start using digital capabilities to transform all aspects of the work, front to back, achieving a step gain in efficiency and productivity and in service experience. As an example, real time easy to use, social-encompassing information across all aspects of business would drive better and faster decision making, at all levels of the organization.

To make sure that most of the opportunities to enhance the operating model are exploited, consistently with the overall strategic goal pursued, banks will also need to consider which level of readiness they have at the moment, and which kind of ambition could be realistically considered given their starting point. In Fig. 2.16 few key examples are given, including the transformation of the customer's journey, the internal decision making and the use and leverage of data and related applications, with indications of what "practitioner", "advanced" or "best in class" would mean—to be considered of course as a moving target as shown in Fig. 2.16—moving targets along the road to banks'.

Chapter 3
An Approach to Bank Restructuring

Abstract In this chapter, an overall, comprehensive approach (the RTX2) to drive the "bankaround" challenge is presented, covering four fundamental phases (mostly complementary, and partially substitute). The restructuring phase—split into financial and industrial—is discussed as it applies to the initial phased of the banking crisis, when the bank is just trying to survive till next Monday, and then over a horizon stretching to few months. It follows (if successful) a turnaround phase, now addressing the business and operating model at a more structural level, and then (again, if successful) a full transformation one, potentially spanning across few years and leading to significant and definite change in the way the bank works and competes in its core markets. In case of failure, or even in case of success and as a complementary measure to be adopted for not viable businesses, the resolution phase—and its last resort liquidation procedure—is finally described at high level.

3.1 Bankaround: The New Game of the Game

Restructuring, resolution, turn around and transformation are the new names of the game in banking and, given the renewed forces at play of global competition, re-regulation, geopolitical disequilibria and, maybe even more importantly, of financial digital (technological, or "fin-tech") innovation, they are here to stay, and grow in importance in the coming years. We are just at the beginning of a disruptive season, in global financial services, and not at the end. It is worthwhile therefore to seriously consider a new way to deal with banking crisis, liquidations and re-birth (or even creation, as completely new business models will emerge from the ashes).

New regulatory regimes, especially in the European Union and building on some of the experiences already developed in the Anglo-Saxon financial markets, are also, albeit indirectly, giving an answer to the questions posed in the beginning of this book (on "whether banks should be let fail, and eventually, how"?):

- Global and regional banks may indeed appear as the next dinosaurs about to be hit by a terminal comet. However, the grim views on their likely or even inevitable disappearance are very simplistic and most likely wrong: many

C. Scardovi, *Restructuring and Innovation in Banking*,
SpringerBriefs in Finance, DOI 10.1007/978-3-319-40204-8_3

financial intermediaries have proved to be extremely resilient and able to change and react. It follows therefore that a first, partial answer would be "banks could need to fail, but some of them have also a chance to change in advance and restructure turnaround and transform to better adapt to the new ecosystem and before getting into serious troubles". Whilst others financial services players could seriously get (or are already) into troubles and with a no return ticket, others could still have a chance to make it, with an holistic approach to industrial and financial restructuring (and not just playing "zombie-like");

- The focus of the questions would then need to be readjusted, as there is a best "how" on letting them fail, and a different best "how" to support their restructuring and transformation (and turnaround—something we will define sits in between, and along a continuum starting from restructuring and going to the final transformation—or resolution). We may call then "bankaround" the new name of the game that will need then a more detailed and methodologically sound clarification. The dinosaurs' tale is not just one of extinction, but also of rapid and discontinuous genetic evolution that will allow the creation of new and stronger species, able to cope with the new ecosystem. Species that, indeed, could allow financial institutions to develop from a "special kind of public utility" companies that need to be saved at all costs, to open market businesses that may need to fail, but have also high chances to grow and thrive in the new global economic order, and with limited systemic risk, should all their survival efforts fail.

If, as we said, restructuring, turnaround, transformation and resolution in banking are still in their infancy—as methodologies and theoretic approach and as a sum (codified or not) of the experience of the practitioners, other best practices need to be learned from other industries, and from the non-financial corporates that already went through "near death" experiences and survived, often via a bankruptcy procedure, or having to liquidate a good portion of their business, but were then able to create and sustain new cycles of value creation and growth.

Hopefully, in the GFS case, this "bankaround" process will also bring to new value creation opportunities, if seen from a private perspective and considering a market-friendly, liberal way of approaching things. And ideally, this "bankaround" process will also be able to bring forward a new global financial order that will be safer and more structurally sound, and better able to contribute to the public good, allocating all the scarce resources (tangible and intangible, and not just financial) that we have in more efficient and effective ways.

3.2 The Unfolding of a Financial Crisis in Three Steps

Before addressing the question of what the best "bankaround" (from both a theoretical and a pragmatic point of view) framework could be, it is useful to go back to the beginning of the banking crisis journey, i.e. at the moment when a new comet

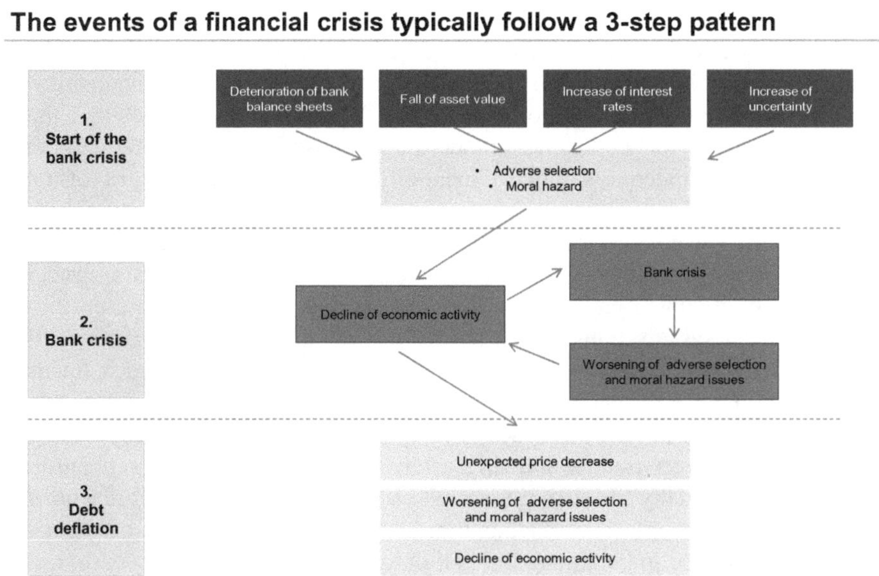

Fig. 3.1 The three main waves of a financial crisis

hits the ecosystem, with a number of destructing waves impacting the financial markets and their main banking intermediaries, often in unpredictable ways. We may however try to simplify and distinguish three following main waves (or steps), as graphically described in the Fig. 3.1.

The first wave starts when the comet hits the banking planet, usually because of a number of fairly typical causes, including the excesses of financial liberalization, the mismanagement of financial institutions (often connected with management frauds) and the credit "boom" (or hyper growth) that, through excessive risk taking and overly generous lending policies tends to translate into asset bubbles, that keep growing and growing… until they burst—as it was the case with real estate bubble in the United States in 2008, often with dramatic effects of the banks' balance sheet, leading them to big losses and to their potential "technical" default (as defined, for this purpose, by a level of regulatory capital falling below the minimum required Law to operate).

If banks fail, and no other short term easy solutions (e.g. merger with stronger banks, or market recapitalizations) are available, the "safety net" provided by the regulators and policymakers steps in, still in the first wave, but that is as much part of the solution as it is part of the original cause—because it incentives the "moral hazard" from the side of the banks and of their managers and boards: as they know, the reasoning goes, that a safety net will ultimately be available, they are keen to take more risks than what should be advisable.

The burst of the bubble, and the following fall in the price of the assets whose price was inflated by the excesses of the lending supply, originates then a phase of deleveraging of the banks' balance sheet—as they have to rebuild their regulatory capital base, weakened by the credit losses—and, as a consequence, a decrease or sharp contraction in the lending supply. This in turn impacts on the availability of new funds and on their relative costs, damaging the profitability and posing a threat to the sustainability of the business model of a number of large to mid corporate, small business counterparts, not to mention the consumption pattern of retail clients.

The second wave then kicks in, as the deterioration of the banks' balance sheet quality turns into a real insolvency (the "technical" default becomes a structural "failure/impossibility to pay"). This, given the strong interlinkages present in the global financial system, translates in the feared "domino effect" or "Herstatt risk" (named after the small German community bank that almost created a financial meltdown in the Country and in the international financial markets, because of the closely interconnected interbank money market).

The domino effect is then showing a tendency of becoming a "self-fulfilling prophecy", as it usually translates in market panic, given the usual over reactions of the media and the people. It could then turn into "bank runs"—the fear of contagion means that you want to be among the first ones to get your savings, in cash, out of your bank, until there is cash in its coffins as the bank will ultimately run out of it pretty fast, giving the implicit multiplier—for any euro of capital there are on average 20/30 of loans—and the duration mismatch—the asset side of the bank's balance sheet is longer dated on average than the liability side—usually of a factor of 3-5X.

And, as the implicit and unavoidable leverage and duration mismatch of the banks' balance sheet imposes the fire sale liquidation of most of the assets owned by the bank (in order to honor the bank's obligation to give deposits back to customers upon their request, e.g. almost in real time, if they ask), this gets translated in further losses and in further reduction of the regulatory capital, and thus in further deleveraging required.

In such a "nothing is left to lose" situation, the bank's own stability, and that of the overall global financial system, becomes further and further unmanageable—adverse selection is reinforced by panic, and moral hazard by the irrational behavior of markets and people, that tends to overshoot in all kind of crisis or fast paced change situation (either translating into too much exuberance, or into a too pessimistic view). The overall negative impact on the economy then gets just worst and worst, with huge losses (and noticeable "migrations") of value.

In the third wave, if the decrease in the price is particularly strong, the crisis can become more severe and become long lasting and structurally "engrained" in the overall economy, as the price reduction affects negatively most of the sectors, whilst liabilities—less sensitive in the short run—are staying stable, if not increasing because of the higher cost of funding (they may decrease in market value, but just because of the loss in the creditworthiness of the bank that has to honor them—this effect and a peculiar accounting rule made possible, in a very illogic way, during the financial crisis of 2008, for global investment banks to record significantly reduced losses because of the—somewhat artificial—"profit" coming from the loss in the market value of their traded debt instruments: as Lehman was approaching default its debt stockpile deep dived.

Adverse selection and moral hazard phenomena thus become the norm in the market, as anybody trusts nobody anymore (as in the famous example of the reseller of used cars) and given the "little to lose" situation of the many, big, speculative bets are becoming the norm and tends to become rationally and even morally accepted.

Then, from a macroeconomic perspective, two quite different scenarios would potentially and finally kick in. In a more "traditional" scenario, and as part of the banks' safety net, the governments would basically refinance themselves (after having bailed "out of troubles" a number of financial institutions and having deployed all kind of expansionary fiscal policies to let the economy stabilize) by printing money—actually sponsoring and allowing their central banks to do it through the full array of technical ways available. Inflation would then ensue, deflating the real value (e.g. in real, purchasing power parity terms, as opposed to nominal ones) of their public debt and other financial obligations (e.g. pension systems etc.). And the inflation would also act as the magic touch able to strongly reduce the liabilities' value of banks, whilst strengthening the value of their troubled assets (e.g. as most non-performing loans are backed by real estate assets, they will grow in nominal value and defend better their purchasing power parity—PPP—value, thus allowing a greater percentage of recovery versus the gross nominal value accounted in the banks' financial statements (normally recorded at historical value). Obviously, an analysis based on the net present value would show very different conclusions.

Apart from "repairing" the book value of non-performing assets, the inflation would also support the recovery of the banks' net interest margin (as their reprice of interest rates are usually faster on the asset side, and much slower and smaller on the liability side). Obviously, because of the macroeconomic mess that would ensue after a high inflation or hyperinflation, there would be huge losses of productivity, and the impairment of real growth drivers and a significant misallocation of resources—not to mention the "unfair" migration of wealth.

The second scenario would however be even more devastating for the overall fabric of the markets and society alike, and not even helping to mend the financial and accounting issues of banks. We are obviously referring to the deflationary scenario that is actually unfolding in the European economy and with a very well-known negative precedent dating back to the "lost decade" experienced in the '90s by Japan. In a deflationary scenario, in fact, lower prices would incentive the postponement of the investment and consumption choices of firms and individuals, and would further exacerbate the losses in the banks' balance sheet and therefore damage their overall profitability (with commissions decreasing as per the asset under management and because of the overall lower activity taking shape at the level of the global economy, and with the interest margin also contracting—it is difficult to price a large spread in a world characterized by negative interest rates—as it is now happening).

With specific reference to the current macroeconomic scenario, as the central banks will start to act in an almost unchartered world, their untested "unconventional" policy making and the reaction of the markets and societies at large could also imply new negative surprises, with further pressure on the stability of the banking system.

3.3 Credibility Is Everything, and the Three Capitals

Paraphrasing Oscar Wilde well known "witticisms", we could argue that "the banker that has credit should ask for no credit at all". In fact, credit should just flow to him (meaning the ability to get funding and then to be able to extend new lending lines to worthy counterparts). In fact, the opposite is most often the case—with credit worthless clients flooding unworthy bankers of new requests for loans and various financing options. More than credit, in fact, credibility is the basic foundation of banking, and of the banks' capacity to survive and thrive—as they are managing an highly leveraged business built on risk and on few other intangible factors.

Credibility is everything in banking, and can mean different things (often apparently inconsistent, but well interconnected) with regards to different people (or stakeholders):

- To regulators, it refers to the credibility that a bank has to demonstrate in its ability to comply with international and local regulations and be "safe and stable". A credible bank reports credible facts and figures, valuing its assets and liabilities prudently and managing risks in a safe way;
- To bondholders, it means that a bank is credible in its promise to repay in full its financing obligations, either senior or subordinated, without engaging in moral hazard that could positively skew the risk/return profile at the advantage of shareholders, but at the expense of debtholders;
- To shareholders, it means that a bank is credible in executing its stated industrial plan, reaching ambitious and competitive profitability and value creation targets (and paying high and stable dividends through time), along a time horizon consistent with their holding period and given the risk/return preferences;
- To employees, it means that a bank is credible in ensuring a stable, if not rewarding and stimulating platform for their personal and professional growth and financial remuneration. And that it is not pursuing aggressive redundancy targets for its short term profitability at the expense of its "human capital";
- To customers, it means that a bank is credible in delivering its promised (and compelling) value proposition, and in managing the personal information of the client, and in handling its savings and overall financials, acting in absence of conflict of interests, or managing them carefully when unavoidable;

- To suppliers, it means that a bank acts in a faithful and consistent way, managing contractors at arm's length, but also without taking advantage of privileged, quasi oligopolistic positioning and being open to long term cooperative partnerships, and respecting the main terms of contracts and payments.

This credibility is the first and more important line of defense against bank runs, and—apart from being required to just "open up the shop every single business day", it leads to the build-up of a number of other tangible and intangible capitals—that in turn contribute to the valuation of the bank of today and (as represented by its goodwill) of the one of tomorrow—with the market value of the bank ideally representing their sum.

For the "bank of today", the "financial capital" values the company's portfolio of financial assets and liabilities (and its net worth), with a greater (positive or negative) premium or discount assigned to it given the "credibility" in the numbers representation offered by the top management, not to mention its perceived ability to manage well those assets in the day to day business of the company. From a "bankaround perspective":

- The limited transparency on sub/non performing and so called "toxic" (structured, highly leveraged and very complex) assets, can contribute to a bigger discount on the nominal value of the net worth, whilst the creation and segregation and ring fencing of a bad bank could help a lot with this regard;
- The weakening of the balance sheet quality and of the solvency ratio (or an higher "Texas ratio"—net non-performing loans over regulatory capital) could lower the solvency ratio of the bank and increase its overall cost of funding, if not preventing its ability of getting any funding at all.

For the "bank of tomorrow", the "franchise capital" values the company's portfolio of client relationships and its breath and depth of competitive offerings that should also translate in a more rewarding pricing strategy (as the brand value grows, the bank should be able to reprice upward its offerings). From a "bank-around perspective":

- The loss of credibility with customers (directly) or with regulators, suppliers, employees etc. (indirectly) could negatively impact on the brand equity and on the franchise capital of the company. A bank in trouble is a "brand in trouble"—and viceversa;
- In more extreme cases (e.g. in break up or partial wind down/liquidation situations), the commercial value tied to having a single or multiple distribution networks also vanishes, as also the loss of specific businesses or geographies could harm in a compounded and often uncontrollable way.

Finally, also the "knowledge capital" impacts a lot on the value of the bank of tomorrow, as any company is at the end made of people (talents and normal workers, still required to have it functioning in a smooth and effective way) and of know how—methodologies, approaches, processes... but also data and information and the IT system required to derive workable intelligence from them, and to get

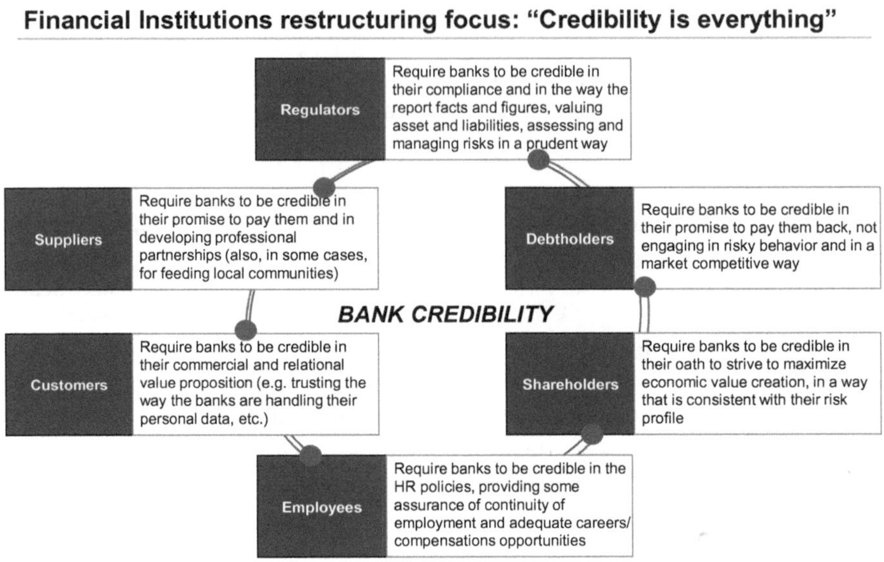

Fig. 3.2 Credibility is everything

then to some kind of sustainable competitive advantage. As people can walk away, also knowledge capital could do in a "bankaround" situation:

- The implosion of the "soft dimension" (linking very different people to the same mission, and letting them work in the same direction) can bring to the diaspora of the talents (the more volatile, high switchers and usually first to fly in case of difficulties), and to the displacement of main organizational settings and levers;
- Also, even the data and information, and the technology required to process them, could get lost or even misappropriated by third parties in situation of distress and for many different reasons, including IT disruptions and human failures to comply, thefts and other forms of misconduct.

The virtuous circle of credibility, encompassing six different stakeholders and with many interlinkages among them is then summarized in Fig. 3.2.

3.4 The "Bankaround" Approach, or RTX2

In our suggested framework to plan and execute a successful "bankaround" we have considered up to four different phases, as graphically depicted in Fig. 3.3, ideally exhaustive and potentially not exclusive: in most of the cases, two-three of them are in fact considered in short succession by banks facing a significant solvability and profitability crisis; in fewer cases just one or the full four; and some

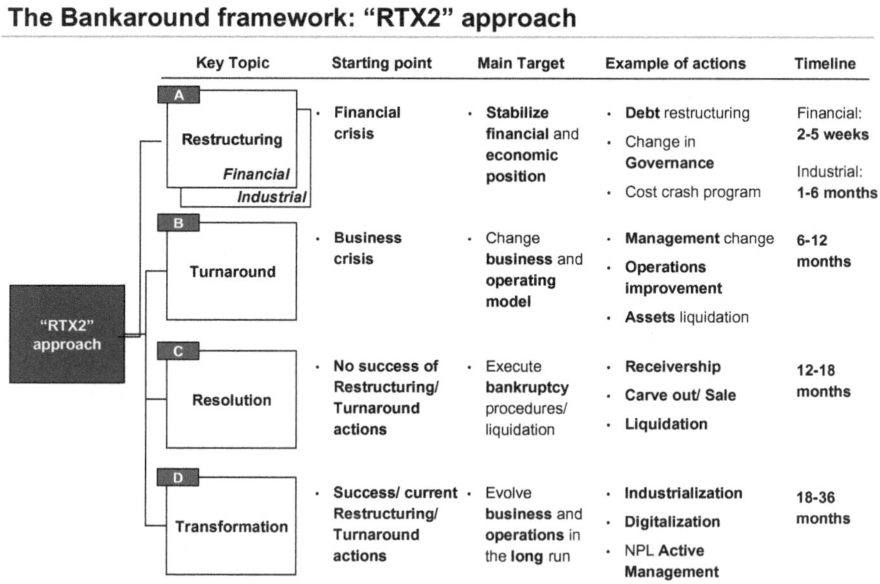

Fig. 3.3 Bankaround or RTX2

overlapping or blurring boundaries is usually found in practice. We will provide a short description in the following paragraphs.

3.5 Restructuring

The first phase of "restructuring" (the first "R") entails mainly with the starting point of the bank's crisis, and has usually two components—e.g. a financial and an industrial one, with the first one (financial restructuring) focusing on the liquidity management component mainly, to make sure the bank has enough cash to manage its immediate needs and duties, including the likely withdrawal requests of panicking clients that will start queuing at its branches. Closely linked with the liquidity issue, the maturity mismatch, or ALM—assets liabilities management—is also addressed by this, with a varying degree of urgency (starting from the next time buckets).

Apart from the liquidity issue, but obviously correlated with that, the bank has to manage an immediate solvency problem (the regulatory capital will likely be at a level below the minimum regulatory requirement, if not from an accounting point of view, most surely from a mark to market point of view). Differently from the liquidity issue, this is not something that can be sorted out in a week end, but that needs to be addressed engaging with regulators and starting considering all kind of financial options to raise capital in the short run. Such options could include a "cash" call from existing shareholders that are able to sustain a short term capital increase, or the intervention of a financial sponsor (private equity or hedge fund), or the sale of assets that could reduce the risk weighted assets, the leverage and the overall size of the asset/liability duration mismatch or (and) the immediate realization of some needed capital gain that may still be embedded in the bank's balance sheet.

All these actions are regulatory capital accretive, even if (usually) they are reached at the cost of a high dilution of existing shareholders (even in the case of asset sales, as they are reached at the cost of a significant discount). In turn, both the liquidity/duration mismatch targets and the solvency ones may have an effect on the profitability of the bank—realizing "fire sales" of assets to increase the cash on hand and to reduce the risk weighted assets and the leverage tends to imply deep discounts, that in turn erode the normal profitability of the bank and therefore the very same equity capital base that is trying, if not to optimize, to preserve.

As a final comment, it is important to note that the timeframe and the scale of the effects of this liquidity/maturity mismatch/solvency/P&L crisis are much more severe and accelerated in a banking environment than in a corporate one. In the worst case for a corporate, the company could end up not being in a position to pay suppliers and employees and to repay their bank loans. But for a bank the worst case would be much worst, with the impossibility of refinancing its balance sheet overnight and the possibility of being put out of business completely, by the depositors run to its branches and ATM machines—with a panicking crisis likely transforming itself into social unrest and violence, given the role and mission of the banking system in any Country—to preserve people's savings and allow them to consume each and any single day, concluding commercial transactions that are absolutely fundamental for the running of the economy and of the civil society.

All in all, we may reasonably argue that financial restructuring for a bank entails a lot of poker-facing acting and gaming, where the bank managers try to preserve the credibility with its clients and banking counterparts ("everything is fine, your savings are safe and well protected" and "you can trade with us, we are as safe as gold, and so is the rest of the system"), and to scare the regulators and politicians, but also proposing to them a clear exit plan ("if you let/force us to go down it will be a mess, that will reverberate across all banks and the overall economy and fabric of society"… but… "we have a plan to get out of this quickly, just give us some help—emergency liquidity lines etc.—and time to execute few asset sales that will put out bank back in shape").

A possible framework on financial restructuring is then shown in Fig. 3.4.

Industrial restructuring is also very important, as it is deployed in the first few weeks and following months of the crisis, even if it is clearly less critical and unique for the bank versus any other company in the world. As a starting point, the industrial restructuring is aimed at making sure that some "operational continuity" is ensured (if the banks' clerks walk away, nobody is opening its branches for business… and if the IT and operations outsourcing suppliers are not paid or at least called to extend their due payments, the system could go down for days, with great

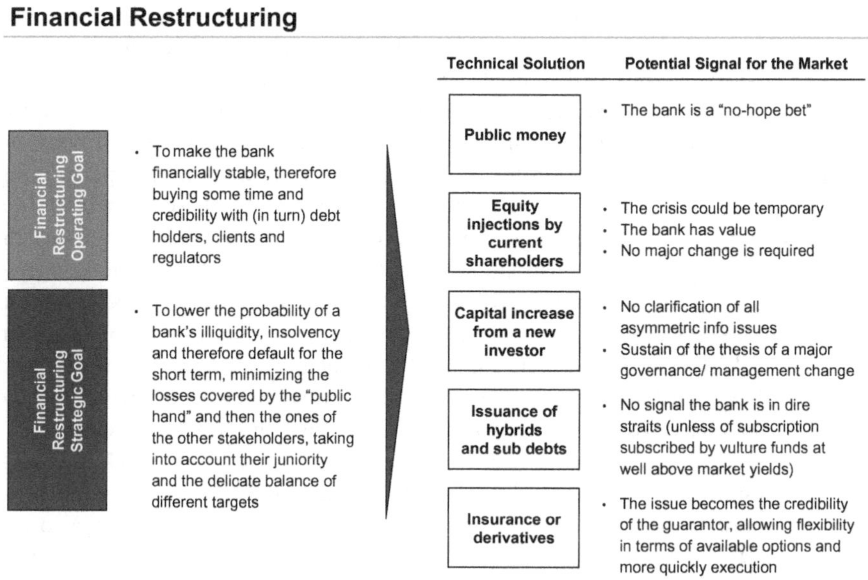

Fig. 3.4 Financial restructuring: a possible framework

disruption of the business and potentially big legal liabilities… if the security services, both physical and digital, are not assured, the remaining money of the bank could literally walk away, etc.).

Apart from this "continuity" issue, some "discontinuities" with regard to the main causes that almost led the bank to the brink of failure are obviously in need. If the financial restructuring's main overarching task is, literally, to survive over the week end and then during the first few weeks, the industrial target is stretching the chances of survival from many weeks to few months. A typical timeframe for a financial restructuring could then be planned for as short as few days/one week, and up to one/two months, with the industrial restructuring being slightly longer and up to 6–8 months. As such, most of the actions that can be taken even during this timeframe are short term, and usually aiming at the 80–20, or even at the 60–40 (do few things, in a very pragmatic way to get few tangible results as soon as possible and forget the rest). It is therefore important to understand that both financial and industrial restructuring are managing mostly to gain time and reach some kind of stabilization by means of many "sub-optimizations"—as the target of the optimization strategies leading to the maximization of the value of the bank in the mid-long term will almost surely lead it to its premature death!

Content wise, the few, typical things that can be done in weeks or in few months to stabilize a bank entail mostly the realm of credit management and work out and of cost cutting.

On the first topic, almost from day one the bank needs to put in place a "stop the bleeding" approach on its core lending business. Assuming most of the troubles are coming from there—almost inevitably for a retail-commercial bank, and the same reasoning would apply even when the main issues come from the trading book—a complete review of the bank's credit policy needs to be put in place and get operational as soon as possible, e.g. given that there will be no time to rewrite the credit policy, a new credit tsar could be temporarily named, to personally review all new major lending decisions. On the existing portfolio of sub and non-performing loans, a number of urgent and critical actions can also be planned and executed. In a crisis situation, the bank's management could likely end up losing its focus on sizeable loans that need close monitoring and lengthy, ongoing restructuring; or letting loose situations that are already non performing and whose collateral could also quickly loose value in time, or just get stolen or destroyed; or losing focus on quick sales of NPL portfolios that, whilst of a financial restructuring nature, could also in parallel contribute some industrial partnership with the acquirers to help the bank in better recovering the troubled assets remaining on its balance sheet.

On the second topic, if not from day one, certainly from the first week, the bank could start improving its P&L and cash management position by cutting the costs which are more visible and likely to produce results in the short run—to also use these results for communication purposes, to reassure the market on the effectiveness of the restructuring plan, and to make sure that all kind of employees and stakeholders get understood the tough message regarding the dire straits of the company and the required sacrifices that are ahead of them. Far from being naïve, any "crash program" on cost cutting is clearly and knowingly sub optimizing the overall productivity of the resources of the bank in the medium run: some of the cuts will surely backfire and translate in the higher costs of operating risks; others will need to be forgiven in the future, even sustaining higher costs than what were originally taken out; others will simply translate in such lousy service propositions that will need amendments in due course, in order not to waste the most critical part of the commercial goodwill of the bank.

But the overall target is to get "stash of cash" as soon as possible, and few arguments to develop a good story and a credible narrative to win back the confidence of the debt and equity markets (the "cost cure" is also working as a good scare to the employees that are wasting resources, or to whom it would just be more convenient for the bank to lose on a voluntary basis—even if it usually works the other way around, with the talents, enjoying better reputation and greater "job liquidity" in the market place, leaving first).

Having explained the logic and the overall caveat of such programs, it is of course in the good experience and in the professional intelligence of the leader driving the restructuring to understand what it's just outright stupid and potentially too dangerous to accept; and when too much is really becoming too much (in the case of my personal experience at Lehman Brothers time, I think it was good to cut the company cars with drivers, and demote even the managing director to the "economy class". But I also think it was stupid to put a freeze on all kind of flights—including for senior partners and sales people—as obviously the number of clients that are ready to take a flight to see you and seek and do business with an ailing bank is not that great, in my experience). As a general remark, even in the most brutal situations of cost cutting, the leader must always remember that clients, and revenues come first—it's fairly easy to cut costs per se, if you just forget about clients and revenues. But that means we are managing a liquidation, and not a restructuring aimed to get the bank back to a going concern.

It is usually useful to map out all these initiatives on a matrix describing, on one dimension, the ease of implementation, and on the other the potential savings attainable in the short run. In the following tables, we have then summarized a potential short list of "cost cutting/cost take out crash program" items, covering all the main blocks of a bank's cost structure, from operations to human resources and related travel expenses, from IT capital expenditure and maintenance to information and data providers, to procurement on third party spend, to advisory fees related to financial, industrial, legal, compliance and marketing services (with noticeable exceptions granted to the professionals involved in the restructuring itself, as they will pretend to be paid well and first—in general, the price sensitivity on their services is also very low, such is critical the situation: who would start negotiating, when a vital surgery is needed in a case of "life or death"? Who would dare selecting the cheapest surgeon, with a very bad track record or uncertain academic curriculum and professional pedigree?).

A potential approach to a cost crash program is then shown in Figs. 3.5, 3.6 and 3.7.

Finally, from a top management perspective, the financial and industrial restructuring phases could entail the immediate change of some of the top management and the renewal of most of the board members. In practical terms, as the

Industrial Restructuring — Crash Program Example (1/3)

Main initiatives — not exhaustive

	Initiative description	Initiative ID
Organization	• **De-layering and increase of span of controls** –E.g. reduce duplications of roles and decrease number of MDs –E.g. Reduce/ freeze promotions and exit low performers	1
	• **Reduce/eliminate potential staff function duplication (e.g. HR, Finance, ...)**	2
HR costs	• **Freeze salary raises and cut bonus compensation** –With the option to use bonus compensation lever to retain only top performers	3
	• **Optimize services for recruiting, especially if outsourced** (e.g. in alignment to potential hiring freeze/ reduction)	4
	• **Reduce external trainings providing only the mandatory ones** –Eventually leveraging on internal resources to prepare in-house courses	5
Travel Expenses	• **Impose stringent budget** –E.g. use of video calls –E.g. setting caps on meal expenses/ client entertainment	6
	• **Reduce travel standards** –E.g. eliminate business class for business below 6 hours –E.g. eliminate car-driver services	7
	• **Introduce "no travel week"**	8

Fig. 3.5 Industrial restructuring: a cost crash progam approach (1/3)

Industrial Restructuring — Crash Program Example (2/3)

Main initiatives — not exhaustive

	Initiative description	Initiative ID
IT capital spend and application landscape	**• Review IT projects portfolio and stop low priority/ low justification projects** –E.g. analyze project portfolio vis a vis the new strategy and re-focus spending on few key transformational projects	9
	• Rationalize license contracts and renegotiate –Applying a rigorous monitoring process to verify compliance to stricter budgets	10
	• Review application landscape and shut down obsolete/ redundant systems	11
ICT infrastructure and hardware	**• Increase utilization of applications and storage servers** –Data centers consolidation	12
	• Reduce/ eliminate unused LANs and other infrastructure components –Performing a rigorous assessment process of the intensity IT infrastructure is used to reduce redundancies and wastes	13
	• Reduce demand of IT services and hardware –Implement 1 PC / workstation per user policy –Reduce maximum mail box size limits –Remove personal printers –Reduce the number of color printers/ print on double face	14
Info/ data providers	**• Review and rationalize info provider services** –E.g. reduce number of Bloomberg/ Reuters licenses, newspaper subscriptions, data/ intelligence units, ...	15

Fig. 3.6 Industrial restructuring: a cost crash progam approach (2/3)

Industrial Restructuring — Crash Program Example (3/3)

Main initiatives — not exhaustive

	Initiative description	Initiative ID
Procurement and 3rd party spending	**• Consolidate and renegotiate supply contracts** –E.g. request a commercial discount by 3-5% also with retro-active effects –E.g. revise SLAs and quality standards	16
	• Impose the compliance to centralized procurement processes for 100% of spending	17
	• Increase restrictions on spending authorizations –E.g. move one level up in the organization the spending authorization	18
Consulting, legal and compliance services	**• Drastically reduce spending on consulting** –Focus on few key strategic initiatives and stop non value added projects **• Place control on external legal advice budget and impose top down savings**	19
	• Create internal management consulting unit (e.g. by efficiency benchmarking/dedicated monitoring, ...)	20
Marketing	**• Cut sponsoring and marketing events budget** –At least freezing the spending for 2014	21
	• Rationalize marketing campaigns costs focusing on key and strategic initiatives only	22
	• Cut merchandise material spending	23

Fig. 3.7 Industrial restructuring: a cost crash progam approach (3/3)

firing of key people in the bank (starting from the CEO, but usually involving the CFO—chief financial officer, the CRO—chief risk officer, the COO—chief operating officer and the CLO—chief lending officer) happens in a matters of few hours. In such circumstances their initial substitutions takes then the form of "ad interim" appointments of seasoned restructurers—usually advisors, or retired professionals that hop from one restructuring case to another, without looking for a long term job. In fact, it would be almost impossible to find the right new top managers over a week end (or convince them they have this great opportunity to leave their current "safe" job, to join a bank that has a small chance to get to next week as a going concern).

3.6 Turnaround

The financial and industrial restructuring (if successful in keeping the bank alive) needs then to be reinforced and institutionalized through time, with a following "turnaround" phase (the first "T") which is really starting to address more and more the real, structural causes of the business crisis of the company. The time horizon of this phase tends therefore to widens, as the first "stabilization" objective has been realized, and the bank has effectively bought some time (either few months and up to one/two year) to turn around its business model.

The focus of the turnaround can then vary accordingly with the real reasons of the crisis that, at this point in time, should have become clearer, and could include fraud, embezzlement and misconduct (some form of fraud is usually associated with any banking crisis, in most if not all of the cases observed and analyzed by the author—playing either as primary cause or secondary effect). And they are often driven, in the best case, by the desperate but unprofessional and sometimes unethical measures that were put in place by panicking managers that tried to avoid the failure at the very last minute, usually making things worst and losses bigger).

In any case, some common ground for the turnaround phase is easy to identify and would usually cover the further reduction of the bank's cost base, with less immediate impact on the incremental cash flow generated, but more sustainable improvements in the overall productivity of the bank's operating model for the long run. This kind of progressive "operational efficiency/performance improvement" focus has more recently been dubbed "industrialization", as the bank starts looking at other productivity improvement initiatives and best practices that were successfully put in place by other non-financial companies that had, through time, to go through painful "near death" experiences—and survived with a mix of relentless focus on wafer thin operating margins and discontinuous and often dramatic take out and redesign of their operating cost structure.

In Fig. 3.8, we have highlighted a potential seven pillars approach to support the "industrialization" review of the operating model—with initiatives that could start being designed and launched during the turnaround phase (starting from the one more radically contributing to the cost cutting for the 1–2 years horizon) and potentially getting into full fruition during the transformation phase, usually encompassing a 2–5 years wider horizon. As described below, these seven pillars,

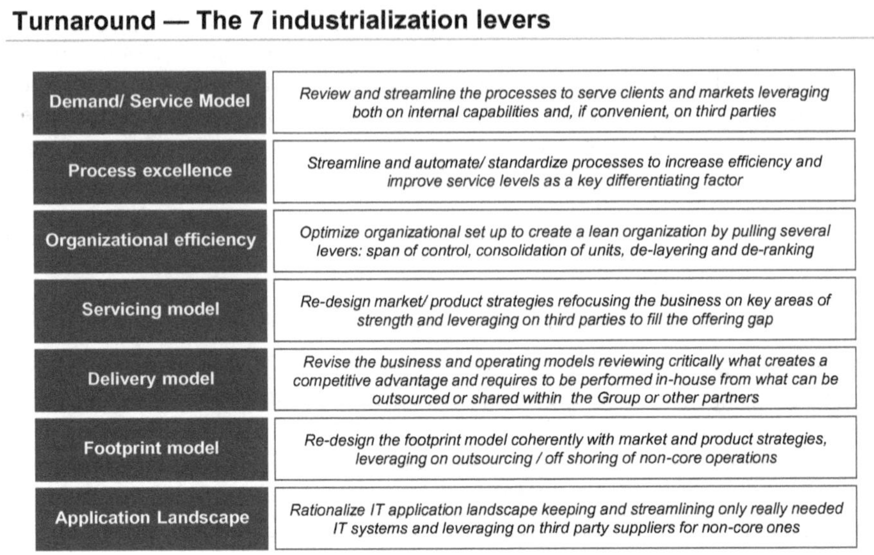

Fig. 3.8 Turnaround introducing an industrialization approach

more structural initiatives are mainly aimed at driving efficiency at the operating model level by fostering standardization, economies of scale, and a more rational approach to the allocation, usage and internal pricing of the "scarce (and costly) resources" used up by the bank to support and develop its business model. The industrialization is in fact also aimed at creating transparency internally, and at sponsoring a continuous benchmarking with the market, in terms of costs and level of the services provided by third parties—potentially suggesting externalization opportunities (including carve outs of specific components of the operating model, to be sold and outsourced to independent BPO—business process outsourcers—as part of the overall transformation plan to come.

A turnaround approach introducing an industrialization approach is then shown in Fig. 3.8.

Of course, there are a number of other industries that are well placed to be used as an inspirational benchmark for the redesign of the banking operating model. At times, the automotive one, and its relentless focus on lean management/six sigma approach, has been mentioned as one of the most effective—with the Toyota approach being one of the very best cases. In other cases, retailing has been used, as an example of efficiency/efficacy in distribution, and telecom and media as an example of "virtual factory", driven by significant outsourcing.

A sample of potential initiatives applied to a global financial services group is then shown in Fig. 3.9, leveraging ideas and best practices from the automotive industry and then applied to turnaround and transformation opportunities that may be found in banking.

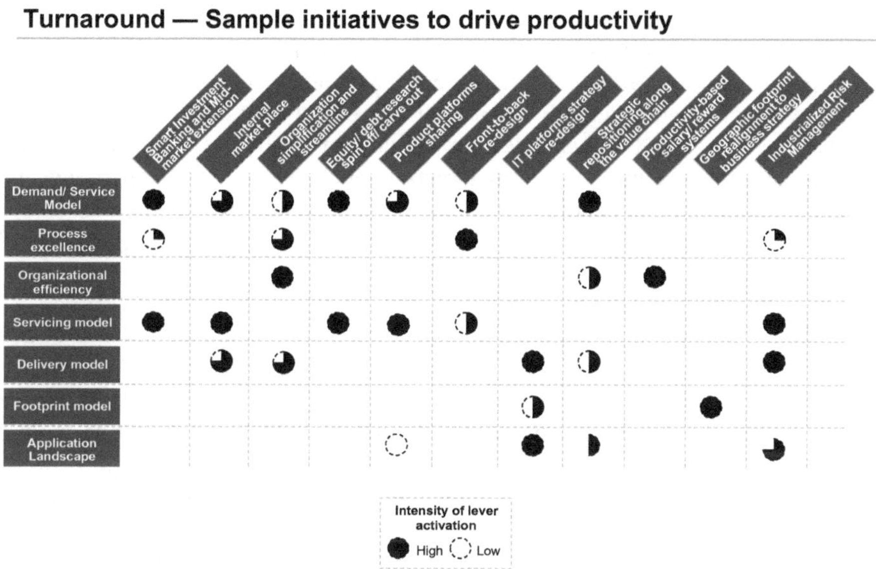

Fig. 3.9 Automotive mindset to drive turnaround and transformation

Finally, as mentioned, from a managerial perspective, the turnaround phase is usually characterized by the progressive renewal of most of the top management positions, after the initial "heavy lifting" and the temporary use of professional "ad interim" restructurers. It is then followed by an organizational overhaul aimed at increasing the speed and effectiveness of the decision making process (a more structured organization, with less concentration of power in few individuals is then considered for the following phase of "transformation").

During this phase, a quick but thorough mapping of the human resources of the bank is also usually performed, and aimed at simplifying the organization and making it leaner (and cheaper), reducing its hierarchical levers, optimizing its span of controls, optimizing its salary bands variations etc. As a by-product of this, a number of redundancies are also further identified, and aimed at having a minimum impact on the working of the organization (whilst surely eliminating a good chunk of costs—two third of the bank's costs are HR related).

As the new management is put in place, some of the general management ad interim roles could then be refocused (e.g. from CEO ad interim to Chief Turnaround/Restructuring Officer, or CBO—bankaround officer, to better distinguish the acronym from the CTO—Chief Technology/Risk Officer). It is in fact in the very interest of the new, "permanent" CEO, to leave the "bad cop" role to an external professional, that does not bother about making a lot of enemies in the organization, and has no conflict of interest with regards her/his future tenure with the bank (that could suggest to cut as few as possible her/his future empire). To the new CEO is then left the task of rebuilding morale, and recreating a cohesive team of managers able to get the bank definitely out of the woods, maintaining and developing a good feeling with all of the stakeholders involved—and with an incentive system that, differently from the CBO (still pretty much incentivized on the "hard" extra cash flow generated for the current period), is increasingly repositioned towards medium–long term targets related to the overall operating and business productivity and capital/dividends generation of the bank.

3.7 Transformation

If the turnaround is successful in getting the bank to an almost back to normal "going concern" state, the full transformation of the bank finally kicks in, with a new management fully in charge and no ad interim or CBO roles still at play for the bank (a CBO may be running in parallel for a while, but then transitioned out quickly).

At a first glance, it may appear that, given the topic of the handbook, and its focus on addressing and solving banking crisis, the transformation (the second "T" of our equation) phase is maybe a bit of a stretch—something to leave for the strategic management consultants, with their usual array of peers benchmarking, competitive repositioning and continuous re-profiling and development of new value proposition. In fact, as discussed at length in the first part of this book, our working hypothesis is that most of the current and future banking crisis will not be (just) driven by the usual array of negative macroeconomic cycle, poor credit underwriting, excessing bets on the trading portfolio and the almost unavoidable mix of misconduct, fraud and money embezzlement, but most of all by the business and operating disruptions brought about by the digital innovation now happening across (inside, as well outside the traditional boundaries of) the GFS, and for most of its fundamental functions—from payments to lending, to insurance, to asset and wealth management, to risk management.

It follows that, no matter how great the restructuring and how perfect the turnaround phases were carried over, the bank could temporarily regain its stability and acceptable profitability, to then jump back to the dire straits of a new crisis as its competitive strategy is just unable to keep track with the latest digital innovation and with the next move of the digital challenger attacking some more profitable parts of the bank's remaining business. Of course, transformation—no matter how difficult it is—could happen successfully and allow to the bank to adapt competitively to the new digital challenges, and to the resurfacing threats of the global macro environment.

The bank's transformation should then really cover many parts of the business and operating model, bringing the "industrialization" of its production and distribution machines to their logical next steps:

- It could for example consider a number of pooling and clubbing options with other peers that may take years to be executed, but are potentially promising to increase significantly the scale of business volumes managed, thus allowing quantum leaps in the productivity of the overall managed cost structure;
- It could consider major carve outs and outsourcing or re-insourcing/repatriation transactions, or other alliances and JV initiatives with other industrial partners, producing something new as a result of this combination and potentially open to offer its services to the open market (by creating a "market utility");
- It could also create other and more profound revisions of the distribution blueprint, or of the existing product portfolios of client segment based service model, thus involving a transformation that starts from the front end and from the client covered and then "lean manage" its way backward to the back office.

But transformation should really entail something more ambitious, deep and permanent, driving the digitalization of the overall business and operating model and a potentially radical strategic review of the very mission and vision of the bank. More than the industrialization, the digitalization would therefore impact the redesign of the overall framework of the operating model, and of the business one, taking into account the changes that are taking place in the market and, ideally, answering to the very simple question regarding "how would I build the bank, should I have the chance to rebuild it from scratch—e.g. without considering all the constraints and treating liquidation costs just as a secondary component of the overall business case, and without necessarily having to proceed by incremental cuts or adds, but considering potential leap frogs".

It is therefore important to conclude that transformation needs to happen from the inside of the organization and in discontinuous waves and with organizational and managerial changes that are consistent with the targeted competitive vision and with the expected new steady state of the markets and societies. But it could also happen from the outside, as the bank is setting up new digital operations and business that are totally separated from the legacy business, or may just decide to buy and merge (or strategically ally with) new digital players. Finally, it is important to remark that transformation happens through time and needs to be sustained over long horizons—it requires therefore more patient capital and long sighted but also very persistent top managers that will most likely have to readdress a number of errors and faulty short cuts made along the way. It is rare in fact the case where transformation is quick and without fault—and just impossible the assumption of an infallible CEO.

A graphical representation of a business plan performance in a typical growth plan versus a "bankaround journey" is then represented in Fig. 3.10—business planning in a RTX2 context.

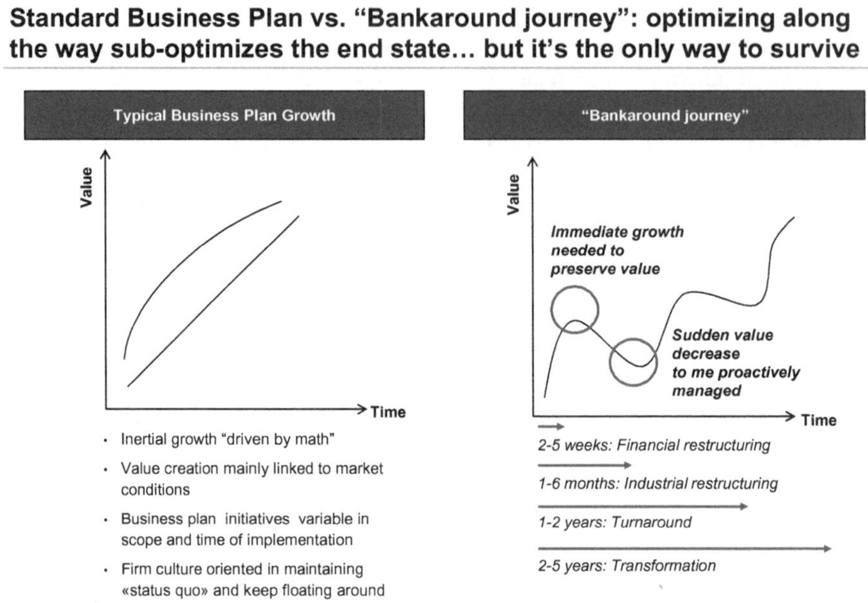

Fig. 3.10 Business planning in a "RTX2" context

3.8 Resolution

In the previous discussion on the different phases towards a full rehabilitation of a bank, we have assumed that everything has gone, more or less, according to plans and the "patient" has survived through the most critical and turbulent phases of the crisis. This is obviously not always the case. And even for some of the most positive scenarios there could be, within the banking group, some legal entity or business unit that are just impossible to recover and keep afloat on a going concern basis. The second "R" of resolution comes then into play, and could unfold in multiple ways, with the implicit aim, as discussed more thoroughly in the next chapter, to keep as much of the bank as possible as a viable business, but also considering alternatively the best ways to manage, via an orderly, transparent and competitive way, the optimal liquidation of the "gone concern" parts.

Resolution, in most of the cases, takes then the form of a receivership, as the relevant regulators (central banks, resolution funds or even the insurance deposit corporations according to the relevant Country and jurisdiction), being already aware of the insolvent status of the bank, are ready to step in and manage the first transition phase of the bank, limiting and ideally avoiding any negative impact on the market. And they can "step in" and start the receivership according to a number of different options and structures—evaluated in accordance with the relevant regulatory background and the magnitude and causes of the crisis that has originated the insolvency.

Even before the actual start of the receivership, changes in the top management and at the board level are sponsored and executed, if not by force of Law, by the moral suasion played by the relevant Institutional authorities. The receiver is then appointed by a bankruptcy court, as a matter of private proceedings, or by a governing body and could refer to a public or quasi-public Institution—specifically for situations where the gravity of the capital gap and the size of the overall assets and liabilities currently managed by the failed bank could have significant negative externalities and systemic impacts on the overall economy and society.

Once the "receiver" sets in, it becomes the ultimate decision-maker and has full discretion in the definition of how the received assets will be managed. The most typical receivership procedure, apart from running and executing a multidimensional "crisis management" to avoid the full collapse of the bank, and defending as much as possible its credibility in the market and its continuity of operations, will start looking for effective ways to reduce the bank's leverage, by packaging assets and selling them at some discount, and by reducing step by step the extensions of the still undrawn credit lines and then getting back as much as possible the loans overdue by clients. Following this process, in the best cases, it will become possible to carve out most of the operating company perimeter, or certain, sizeable businesses as "good bank", to be sold in a competitive proceeding and with a minimum amount of capital, but already "cleaned" of the most trouble assets and of the contingent, major risks that could still be address in the remaining shelf of the bank, or in another, well defined portion dubbed "bad bank"—definitely run for the most optimal liquidation, in the timeframe allowed by circumstances.

Whilst the resolution "phase" will be addressed in more detail in the following chapter, the relevant point for this discussion is about this second "R" being an integral part of the overall "bankaround" integrated approach, as some liquidation—orderly, transparent, competitive and with minimal systemic impacts—will very likely be required in most cases, for the good of the remaining going concern business, for the maximization of the economic value involved and for the sake of the general good being pursued by the "creative destruction".

3.9 The Citigroup Case Study: Avoiding Nationalization at All Costs

Citigroup, one of the biggest and more international of the global banks was born out of a bold serial acquisition strategy that culminated with the mega merger of Citicorp (mainly active in the mortgage and credit cards business) and Travelers Group (mainly active on the life and P&C insurance sectors). The Citi "umbrella" logo came, in the early '90, to exemplify the "one shop stop" offer (all financial products and businesses were offered under the same umbrella brand and could almost be bought in the same shop, from consumer finance to retail and commercial banking to insurance and asset management to investment banking).

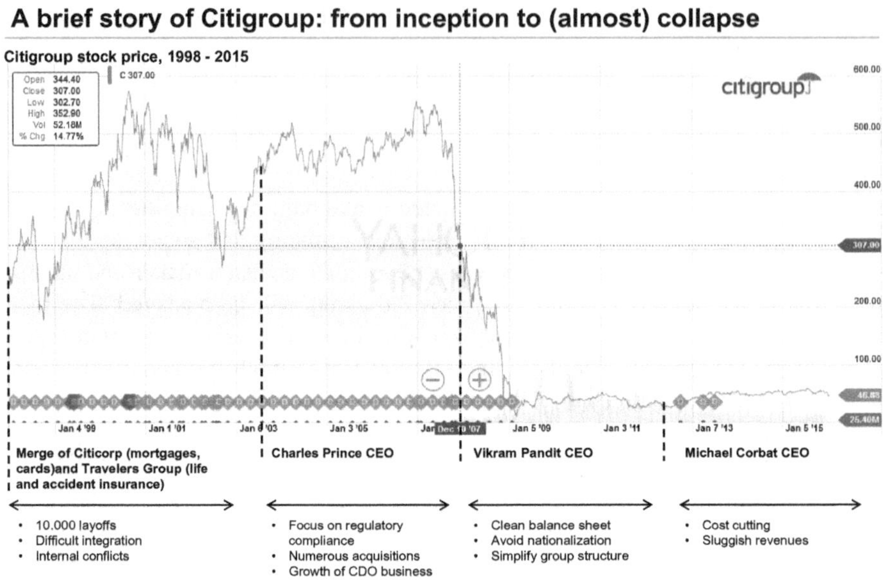

Fig. 3.11 Citigroup: the collapse

Notwithstanding the difficult integration of the different entities, the painful layoffs and the internal management conflicts (made all but more likely by the different cultures and background of the people now making up the big banking group), Citi—under the leadership of the CEO Charles Prince—came to epitomize the successful global US based bank, potentially able to cover the globe and follow its most international clients (challenging few other players, namely JP Morgan Chase, also United States based and HSBC, a UK bank but mostly based in Asia).

This successful story came to an abrupt end at the end of 2007, when the poor financial results (first) and the huge losses accumulated on the specific securitization business of the CDOs (collateralized debt obligations) translated into an outright collapse of the stock price (as shown in the Fig. 3.11).

More specifically, the Citigroup mortgage arm become heavily involved and with a long position on the inflated but still growing real estate sector in the US. Moreover, the investment banking arm was also riding the wave of the booming US CDO market, with a total issuance of the collateralized debt instruments that just tripled between 2003 and 2005, from 7 to 20 Bln USD circa. With the first signs of weakness coming from the real estate sector, Citi kept growing in these businesses, taking even more risks and loading its balance sheet of plain and synthetic positions linked to the performance of the real estate sector, with lax risk management policies, particularly for its over-sized fixed income currency and commodities (FICC) division.

It even kept buying US mortgage players until September 2007, in the belief that the weaknesses were temporary and that the for the real estate sector in America there was just one way (up). Even poor Q3 2007 results on the CDO book (with heavy write downs totaling USD 6 Bln circa) were considered just a short-term, temporary profit slump. But things kept going just on one way (down), as the real estate weakness translated into a market crash followed by a proper bubble deflation. In the coming months Citi had to provide almost 8 Bln USD to a number of SPV (special purpose vehicles) that had bought CDOs and were now unable to pay back even their senior bond holders. A further write down of USD 11 Bln on the CDO book by the end of 2007 lead finally the CEO, Mr. Prince, to resign, with Vikram Pandit, a former hedge fund trader and entrepreneur, taking his role a month later, and starting, in a way, his RTX2 journey—addressing the financial and industrial woes of the bank, whilst doing the utmost to avoid the full collapse and nationalization (being a globally systemic bank) of City.

Pandit's tenure at the helm of Citi was marked by a number of financial and industrial initiatives, and by the creation of a "good bank" and of a "non-core" bank (or "bad bank", just recently dismantled, in 2016), aimed at selling and working out all the many troubled assets and businesses of the former "one stop shop" global bank. From a financial restructuring perspective, Mr. Pandit almost immediately consolidated the off-balance sheet assets (most of them non performing) so as to provide clarity on what was really the size of the mess (big enough to warrant an initial write off of 22 Bln USD in one of the first quarters of the new CEO in charge). In parallel, a capital raise, realized via a private placement with the Sovereign Wealth Fund of Singapore was quickly realized, at deep discount and with a significant dilution for the old shareholders, in order to avoid the public intervention and potential nationalization of the bank. But the coordinated and multiple moves of, separation, clean up and capital raise were not enough to reassure the market, as the stock price of Citi just kept plummeting.

A bailout package, supplied by the US Government, was finally agreed upon in 2008, few weeks later the default of Lehman Brothers. With a preferred stock injection of 27 Bln USD, the US government became de facto the main shareholder of the bank (25 of the 27 Bln USD were later converted into common stock), with an unlimited coverage (through a number of facility lines) of all the losses exceeding USD 29 Bln and an hard clause to stop paying dividends until the bank had restored its financial viability and some kind of industrial core profitability. In fact, on the industrial restructuring and turnaround side, Pandit was quickly targeting a reduction of more than 53,000 employees in the Citi workforce, and the rapid turnaround of many non-profitable businesses, or their outright sale to third parties, even if achieved with huge discounts versus their historical book value. Particular care was also given to the creeping IT system, a jigsaw resulting from too many mergers and too many legacy systems that had never been fully integrated, that eventually made things even more difficult for the already lax internal risk management system. A significant number of changes at the top management level, a reorganization of the group and a new risk management system were also achieved by Pandit.

In the end, as the US market, contrary to the European one, started to recover few years later, and with the benefits coming from Pandit restructuring and turnaround program, the US government unlimited insurance was never actually used—it performed well in terms of back stop in the mind of market participants, that were convinced that Citi could never go under as the US Country was behind it. And the government ended up selling its stake in Citi with a profit in excess of 11 Bln USD.

Having tried to avoid being nationalized, and having failed, Citi was now again fully private and profitable in the first quarter of 2009. But as the restructuring and turnaround plan had been proving, at the end, quite successful, the real transformation of Citi was still taking time to materialize and produce financial results. As the bank was failing repeatedly to take off once and for all, new tensions mounted with the CEO and with the institutional shareholders, bringing to a new CEO, Michael Corbat, at the helm of the bank in 2012. Financial results kept being sluggish for a few years, and then started to pick up in 2015, with the stock price repeatedly beating analysts' expectations, with the materialization of some transformation of the core businesses remained within the "umbrella".

Why did Citigroup get into a mess in 2007? Was it just because its over-reliance on the real estate sector in the US? Or was it due to its over-acquisitive strategy of the past? Had it become not just too big to fail, but also too complex to manage? Since the unlimited bailout insurance provided by the US government was not used in the end, could it be considered a useless and costly burden for the bank in those years? And what were the costs and the potential benefits of avoiding at all costs the nationalization? Was the parallel financial and industrial restructuring operated by Pandit enough to pursue the stabilization of Citi? Or a more profound and extended separation of a good and bad bank should have been considered? And a more radical exit from businesses that are still unprofitable 5 years later? What were the management style differences of Pandit versus Prince, and versus Corbat, the new CEO? How diverse was their mission and how contingent was their fate on the real estate market trajectory? Is their expected and optimal set of technical and managerial skills consistently and radically different? From an industrial perspective were the moves pursued by Pandit enough to survive? And prosper? Which kind of different time frames could he have considered to launch parallel initiatives? And was in general such a plan just trying to resolve, backward looking, some issues of the past? Pandit resigned in 2012, after shareholders rejected his compensation request of 15 Mln USD—hiring subsequently Corbat with a compensation package of 14.5 Mln USD. Were investors justified for being discontent with Citi's lack of growth and subdued profitability in the years up to 2012?

3.10 The Hypo Real Estate Case Study: The State Footing the Bill

HypoVereinsBank (HVB), a mid-sized German bank, was originally set as a universal bank with a mortgage lending focus. In the early 2000, it faced then insolvency, because of its risky lending business operated on East German property.

Hypo Real Estate (HRE) was then spun-off from HVB in 2003, cleaning its mortgage book by selling most of its NPL in the domestic market. In 2007, just in the wake of the upcoming global financial crisis, HRE bought Depfa Bank, an Irish public finance lender, operating in the US with high leverage and with high asset liabilities mismatches (as common in the public finance market due to the perceived high quality of the assets and counterparts, and given the long durations of the infrastructure projects being financed).

After the acquisition of Depfa, the group reached a leverage ratio of 68, with an equity to assets ratio of 1.5 % (the leverage of Depfa was originally even higher, approaching 120 in 2005). Then the global financial crisis started to hit just few months after the Depfa purchase, making Hypo unable to refinance its long term debt mainly backed by real estate collateral. The bank was however able to accumulate Euro 100 Bln of short term, unsecured loans mostly coming from local Institutions from the Munich area. The Greek crisis, hitting the public debt market and hinting for the first time at the idea of the risks being shifted from the private market to the balance sheet of Countries, made then things much worse, as Depfa was holding Greek government bonds and overall the spreads on public debts started to widen—implying significant losses on the books of HRE.

Also, after the Lehman's debacle, the unsecured lending market shut down almost completely, making impossible to HRE to refinance its short term unsecured funding structure. Just to stay afloat, HRE was forced to ask a Euro 50 Bln loan from the German State and further guarantees for 30 Bln circa. A Law was then hurriedly passed to potentially force a squeeze-out and take over of the bank by the Government. Despite this, the government made a "shareholders' friendly" offer, that was however refused. As the initial public funds were not enough, the government had then to extend a further Euro 50 Bln. Failing that as well, in 2009 the government finally forced its hand and nationalized HRE, after injecting a further Euro 6 Bln of equity—a bad bank was then created in 2010, generating losses in excess of 13 Bln. But any bail-in, even of subordinated debt, was averted, as the German federal government kept footing the bill—with regulations still allowing this at the time.

Was the original business model of Depfa low or high risk, and under which conditions? And was mixing the public finance business with the real estate lending one creating diversification or an even greater stretch of long dated maturities and thus risk concentration? Was, in any case, too much and too early to absorb by HRE? Was this, eventually, the right decision, in terms of pushing for the full clean up and restructuring of the bank, or it just delayed a process that would have been more effective and decisive if driven by private investors and with some debt holders "burning their fingers" in the meantime? Should the government have therefore prioritized any debt conversion opportunities or new private equity capital, even if at the cost of huge write downs and some losses to subordinated debt holders? And was the "forced hand" assumption of control by the government, obtained via ad hoc Laws and some harms twisting, the right thing to do, given the obstinacy of past shareholders to refuse any government intervention? How would have the whole process played, should had this happened just few years later, with the new bail-in law into place and the escalated sensitivity, at the level of the European Union, vis a vis any kind of direct State intervention and for any kind of direct/indirect State aid?

Chapter 4
A New Resolution Regime in the European Union

Abstract In this chapter, a more in depth discussion on the new resolution regime developed and now being implemented in the European Union is presented—a description of how the single resolution regime is working and how it interacts with the resolution fund is also described. Starting from the discussion of the safety net mechanisms, the "bail-in" rule, as opposed to the "bail-out" one is then presented and discussed with few noticeable cases, and considering the potential implications on the overall approach: how it could make the "bankaround" challenge more effective and efficient but also potentially more destabilizing at the level of the fabric of society. Also, the implications of the shareholders, as opposed to the debtholders and to the tax payers are discussed. Finally, the characteristics of the emerging leader of a bankaround is discussed at high level, showing the many winning traits she/he should possess in order to manage successfully all the main phases of the RTX2 approach.

4.1 A Safety Net to "Let Them Fall Safely"

It is not uncommon to find, at least in Europe, some kind of safety net aimed at supporting the most critical national champions, across a large number of so called "strategic" industries that are deemed to have some specific relevance and or national interest, because of their size (e.g. contribution to GDP), the products they do (e.g. defense) and the number of people (and therefore voters) they currently employ. But it's basically just for the banking sector that such safety nets are becoming very widespread and far reaching, and institutionalized with regulatory protocols that have also been agreed and negotiated with other major economic zones. And not just because of the regulators willingness of preserving the "level playing field", but mostly out of the fear that because of the high level of interconnectedness existing among international banks and financial markets, any local crisis could easily and quickly turn into a global one.

C. Scardovi, *Restructuring and Innovation in Banking*,
SpringerBriefs in Finance, DOI 10.1007/978-3-319-40204-8_4

Banking is, in a way, a fairly dangerous business, because of its inherent leverage, its asset driven volatility and immateriality. And it is also a politically and socially charged one, as it entails the management of the savings of individuals, the opportunity for many to buy a house that they will repay through time, the access to financial resources for small businesses and corporates and the orderly functioning of many critical "utilities" such as the payments and settlements related to any kind of transaction, from basic consumption to global trade.

It follows that one the overarching goals of policymakers and regulators alike are to guarantee the stability of banks, as prerequisite of the stability of the GFS itself. It's not within the scope of this handbook to discuss which kind of supervisory mechanisms are already in place to prevent a banking crisis, but it is however useful to consider the basic elements of the safety net, as the following discussion on the resolution regime is closely related to them. In short, the safety net can pursue generic or more specific objectives such as:

- The protection of deposit holders and savers in the system, by protecting the trust in the solvability of the system (notwithstanding the intrinsic leverage), and therefore lowering the cost of funding of banks and allowing to them to lock in a longer (behavioral, if not contractually defined) duration on the liability side;
- The reduction of the risk of a bank run by depositors, and of the related social unrest, given the inherent asymmetric information and the different understanding of the banking risk we may assume different counterparts may have in time (with large institutional funds, as well as very rich people, assumed to be more knowledgeable; and with more retail, mass market/affluent and small business clients);
- The reduction of negative externalities on the "real" economy (as distinguished by the "financial" economy: if the lending supply stops, all kind of manufacturing and other non-financial service industries will be impacted, the former generally more than the latter, with significant impact on the GDP growth rate).

However, as a consequence of this safety net, as in the acrobat example (doing riskier and riskier figures when circling up in the air), a very significantly distortion is introduced in the incentive system of the market—the lower probability of going bust can push the banks' top management to pursue riskier and riskier strategies, and the knowledge of the safety net can excuse the clients' lazy attitude, with regard to their knowledge and continuous monitoring regarding the health of their bank (if a perfect safety net exists, customers will go to riskier banks, as they will tend to pay more on gathered deposits, and lend more freely—if not recklessly, to their perspective clients; and customers will keep shopping around not caring about the credibility of their bank).

We may therefore argue that, ideally, as stated in the beginning of this hand book, the safety mechanisms, more than being aimed at preventing any major loss in the system and to protect the more inexperienced and weak, they should aim at letting banks that really deserve to fail to be fail indeed and be liquidated (or, at least in part, restructured and turned around) in a safe way: in an orderly, controlled, transparent and competitive way, e.g. preventing any major disruption into the system, the widespread contagion to worthy counterparts and—therefore—the best reallocation of resources via "creative destruction".

4.2 The Safety Net in European Banking

The safety net in European banking is currently operated on a Country by Country basis, with different levels of effectiveness … as some recent cases have shown: notorious is the case of the UK depositors that invested in current accounts and bonds offering very high yield and managed by Icelandic banks—they lost a lot of money, as not only the banks failed, but the Icelandic safety net was not good enough to plug the whole and the UK one did not apply and could not be operated, as it is driven by the home Country of the failed bank, not of the customers). In terms of deposits insurance, the general rule being applied is that deposits under a certain threshold—100k Euro or Pounds circa—are protected and guaranteed by a public agency or by a private institution that is however under the control of the relevant Ministry of Finance and Central Bank. The public-private Institution is funded on an annual basis by the banks of the system as a share of their deposits.

Also, specific rules and procedures are also defined for allowing a direct intervention of the relevant regulators or of any other public bodies to manage banks in distress that may pose systemic threats to the economy.

The two approaches most broadly utilized so far have been, on one side, the "bail-out" operated by States recapitalizing the failed banks that are posing systemic threats, and the "normal" corporate bankruptcy regime utilized in some instances e.g. the Lehman case) in the US. Other, new forms of "special resolution" are however being developed, most notably in the European Union, with the aim of optimizing the implicit trade-off usually associated between the overall costs to taxpayers and the stability of the banking system (very high, the first and the second, for the "bail-out" operated by the State option; and minimum for the normal bankruptcy regime).

More broadly, these kind of interventions may assume the form of emergency lines extended by central agencies or central banks, and "too big to fail policies", where central authorities consider the potential bankruptcy of a systemic institution as an unacceptable hazard, and therefore are ready to intervene directly, using taxpayers resources (subject to the competition authority's rules forbidding "State aid" and any potential trust issue materially reducing the level playing field and the market's competitiveness that is sought and guaranteed by liberal policies). This direct intervention can then take the form of a direct nationalization of the bank; of an indirect "control room" as managed by the Central Bank for the bail out of a bank that still retains a diverse base of shareholders and its proper governance and management as a private company; or of a public guarantee on the troubled bank's debt that is ensuring its viability in the interbank markets and its ability to refinance its assets.

In the context of the "new, upcoming approach", first and foremost, a new governance for the overall management of the prudential banking supervision has been defined for the European Union member States, covering not just the safety net mechanisms, but also the overall supervision and direct resolution procedures:

- As described in Fig. 4.1, the European system for prudential banking supervision is now made up of a new European system risk board, and by a number of European supervisory authorities, some newly created at European level, interacting with the Country specific central banking structures still in place;
- The board and the authorities are then working together on both macro-prudential topics (e.g. the potential risk embedded in cross currency mortgages, or on fixed rate loans, given changes in the yield to maturity structure), and on micro-prudential situations arising from the specific crisis-hit banking institution.

A synopsis of the new European system for prudential banking resolution is then shown in Fig. 4.1.

The overall frame of prudential supervision is then based on the new design for the European banking union that is taking shape and is being executed on the basis of three pillars:

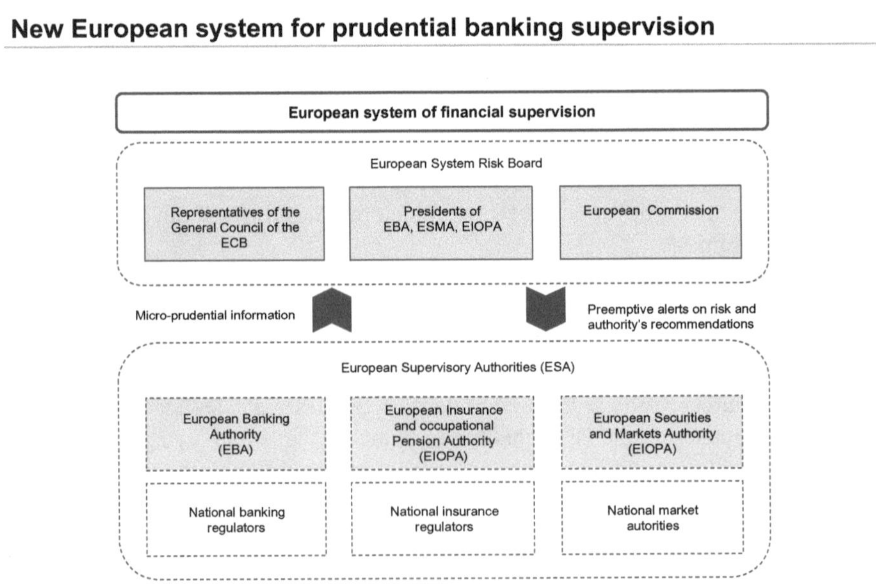

Fig. 4.1 A new European banking financial supervision system

- The first one, the "single supervisory mechanism", is aimed at setting consistent supervisory standards in the Euro area, prescribing (initially) a direct ECB (European Central Bank) supervision activity on the 130 circa largest banking groups in Europe—it will then be extended through time, to potentially cover the full lot in future years. In place since November 2014, its application was preceded by a thorough evaluation of the banks' balance sheets, to set a credible, fair and transparent starting point for comparability and homogeneity of treatment and to recover some of the lost credibility of the system. This first pillar is therefore aiming at a reduction of the regulatory fragmentation of the market, and at improving the transparency and "faith" in the banks' financial statements—even if a number of different accounting, tax and even regulatory treatments (as ratified by relevant local law makers) still persist at domestic level;
- The second one, the "single resolution mechanism", is prescribing a single authority for managing banking crisis and running eventually their resolution. Apart from the standardized processes, and the timely and professional way of working the mechanism is introducing (more along the lines of the "creative destruction" a la Schumpeter), the mechanism can count on the "burden sharing" (conversion into equity of subordinated debt so as to have other hybrid equity underwriters sharing the pains of a banking failure) and on the "bail in" procedures (progressive conversion as loss absorbing of all the remaining part of the liability structure, from the most junior to the most senior, with the sole exclusion of the quota of direct funding below the 100.000 Euro threshold that is guaranteed directly by the insurance fund on deposits). Apart from this "burden sharing" and "bail in" procedures, the resolution mechanism can also count on the capital (Euro 55 Bln circa) contributed by the member States to the Single Resolution Fund, in place since the beginning of 2015, ready to be used to manage even the most complex resolutions in an orderly and not entirely destabilizing way. As the resolution fund is financed pro quota by the State members, it aims to break the vicious circle that usually leads a local corporate crisis to become a banking risk and then in turn a sovereign debt crisis (when the State is forced to step in and close the capital shortfall, to avoid the melt down of the overall financial system, increasing its public debt almost to the point of unsustainability);
- The third one, the "single deposit guarantee", is a third scheme still pretty much under discussion that would potentially target a "one banking market, one deposit guarantee" vision—de facto completing the mutual sharing of "unbearable risks" at the level of the member States. So far, however, just a mild homogenization of the local schemes have been agreed, and with a reactive approach that is still far from the most "active" ones, as played for example by the FDIC (Federal Insurance Deposits Corporation) in the United States. The full unification principle, apart from being questioned by the largest and wealthiest States (that have to contribute with a percentage of the deposits banked in the system) could also be contested on the basis of the "moral hazard" it implicitly introduces and fosters, as the more risk taking institutions will pay a similar price for insuring their deposits and therefore a similar cost of funding,

that will be (at least for the first 100.000 Euro slice insured) equally protected, no matter what the bank's management is doing—therefore not incentivizing the deposit holders to do a proper risk underwriting analysis. Not to mention the different returns applied to the same insured risks, as yields offered will vary.

4.3 "European in Life, and National in Death", No More

For the sake of our discussion on the restructuring, turnaround, transformation (and/or resolution) perspective of the main European banks, and given the aim of better allowing the process of "creative destruction" to take place, the second pillar of the "new" European banking union is the most relevant. In fact, since the beginning of 2015, with the single resolution mechanism in place (SRM), the single resolution board has become the single authority responsible for the resolution, within the single monetary union area, of any bank with relevant cross border activity, and of any other one of the 130 circa already directly supervised by the ECB. The relevant national authorities will then keep being responsible for all the other ones—but within the rules set by the SRM.

In practice, the resolution of failed banks will be financed by the remaining banks of the system and by the shareholders and debtholders of the bank itself. Instead of a "public bail out" (the failed bank being recapitalized by the State and de facto by the taxpayers and therefore "bailed out"), a new "private bail in (the creditors of the bank, for the amount of money above the minimum guaranteed, e.g. 100.000 Euro circa) could be used for the recapitalization—with the debt being converted into equity and progressively being wiped out following a cascade, from the most junior to the most senior—a process that will continue until all the losses are covered and a proper minimum regulatory capital ratio has been reconstituted in full. The conversion of creditors' funds would then need to be equal to at least 8 %, before another back stop facility could be drawn in—we are referring to the Single Resolution Fund that could however contribute up to a maximum of 5 % of the total liabilities of the failed bank. The resolution fund is being initially capitalized for 55 Bln Euro (and is active from January 1st 2016), via bank levies raised at national level and then gradually mutualized in the course of the following 8 years—de facto fully realizing the vision of banks that will be both European in life and… in death as well.

The overall governance of the SSM (Single Resolution Mechanism) and of the SRF (Single Resolution Fund) will be driven by the Single Resolution Board (SRB), based in Brussels, with 6 permanent members (one member appointed by each participant member State), and 2 permanent observers named by the Commission and by the ECB and able by mandate to:

- Draw resolution plans and assess resolvability of banks;
- Implement the resolution of banks;
- Own and manage on an ongoing basis the SRF.

The SRF, with a target capital base of a minimum 1 % circa of the overall deposit base of the banks covered—target that should be reached by 2024—will be funded both ex-ante and ex-post:

- Ex-ante contributions will be calculated by the single banks supervised and raised annually by each member State—they will be determined as a fixed pro rata (given the size of the bank) component, plus a risk adjusted contribution (the more risky the bank, the more it will have to contribute to help in back stopping the system), therefore addressing, albeit in a still imperfect way, the issue of moral hazard distortions;
- Ex-post contributions will then be required in case the SRF sources will not be sufficient and up to a maximum of 3 times the annual contribution—but surely they could be raised should they be not enough;
- Finally, the SRF will also have the possibility to borrow from the capital markets, to introduce some leverage to the overall capital that would be ready to be injected into the system, therefore making the solution even more "private", as the borrowing would have to happen at market terms and in a very transparent and competitive way (we may assume underwriters could include pension funds, insurance companies and asset managers, and not the banks themselves to avoid just a shift of the capital gap).

A summary of some of the most critical interplays happening within the SSM and the SSR is then shown in Fig. 4.2—the SSM and SSR and the second pillar: how they work.

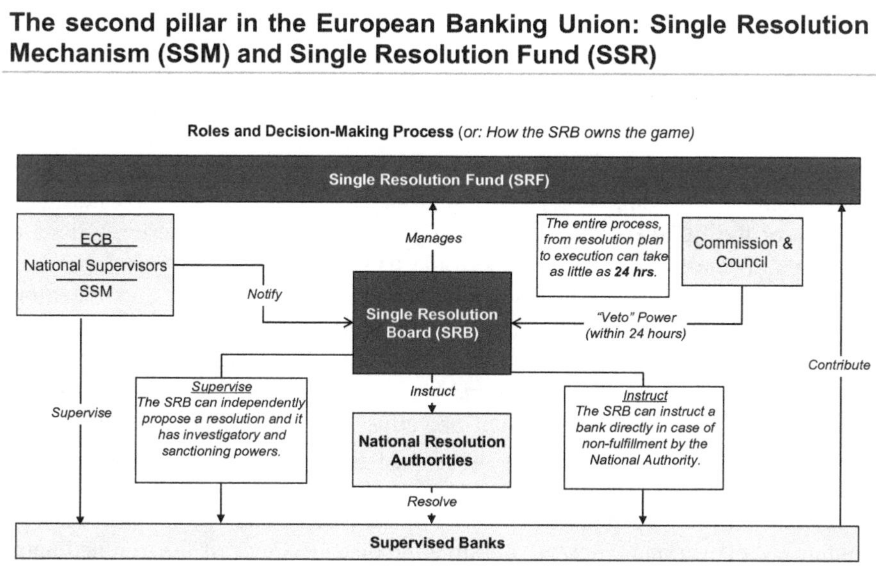

Fig. 4.2 The SSM and SSR and the second pillar: how they work

From a business impact perspective, it will then follow that banks will become now liable of the supporting measures (including heavy restructuring and liquidation procedures) undertaken by the SRF, whatever their nationality and home/host Country/Countries of presence. And the bail in new rule will surely have a negative impact on their cost of funding, as the perception of banks as "impossible to fail" because of their utility functions, potential system impact and national interest will be once and for all translated in an "unlikely to fail".

And in failure, after the equity, the potential losses will reach out fast the remaining of the funding structure, from subordinated debts, to junior and then senior bonds and even sight deposits (above the minimum guaranteed). This "loss absorption" nature of the liabilities, even if nothing new for the world of corporate restructuring, is a major discontinuity in the banking system with very important implications at all kind of levels, including social and political, as the case of Banca Etruria in Italy has recently shown (even if this case was just referred to the "burden sharing" inflicted to subordinated debts—unfortunately owned by both institutional and retail clients, with the Government ultimately stepping into cover the losses of the latter).

From a governance and regulatory perspective, given the centralized and stronger resolution authority that is in the process of being set and operating in Europe, the implications will be felt at the banks level even before the actual start of a resolution process.

In fact, the Resolution authority will have the power to assess preemptively, and without the need of any particular reason, the resolution plans of the banks supervised, and will most certainly increase their investigative and sanctioning powers—usually in liaison with the Central Banks of the home Country.

4.4 Resolution Versus Liquidation

The primary objective of the SRM and SRF is clearly to ensure the overall stability of the system ("safe and sound banking system ..."), ideally reached not at the expenses of the EU taxpayers and avoiding severe and negative repercussions on the competitiveness and transparency of the banking system (e.g. ensuring a level playing field, avoiding State aids and the incentives distortions and the moral hazards for banks top managers to take even more risks in the certainty of the safety net provided, as in the past has been the case when the Governments were ready to step to plug almost any capital hole and "bail out" the distressed banks).

However, a noticeable and implicit objective is also to ensure some level continuity of the financial institutions in distress—e.g. giving them a chance to recover after all. The SRM/SRF are in fact design to allow some kind of "creative destruction" in the economy, with the related reallocation of resources, but avoiding, whenever and wherever possible the disappearance of the troubled banks and of their operating businesses. That's why so much emphasis is given to the "resolution" word, as opposed (or in a complementary way) to the "liquidation" word. A more specific and careful definition of the two is, at this point, needed and overdue.

In the case of a failed or likely to fail bank, the first decision the regulators should be considering regards the opening of a "banking crisis state", should the normal market supervisory activities and specific action plans not be enough to proactively solve the critical situation. On this basis, following the formal declaration of the "crisis state" of the bank and its significant risk of "gone concern", the regulators should consider if the failed or likely to fail bank has a specific public relevance and potential domino effects, or not. In the first case, a resolution procedure is de facto indicated as the only way to go, with the application of the SRM and SRF.

In the second case, the regulators could still consider if the costs of a direct intervention of the resolution mechanisms would in any case be better, also from a financial point of view (because, for example, the cost of deposit insurance would be much higher than the one related to the recapitalization of the bank to ensure its going concern), so as to justify the use of the bail-in and of the other SRF resources (or of the single member State resolution funds, also funded by the banking system, for the smaller banks) to "save the bank".

Alternatively, a more straight forward liquidation procedure can be activated by the individual Central Banks (as this is the case of minor banks, therefore still not supervised by the ECB and most likely not to pose any system risk to the overall banking system), usually starting with the nomination of a liquidator in charge.

The overall aim of a liquidation procedure is then to remove in an "orderly" way (e.g. avoid panic, negative side effects in the markets, but also speculation and market cornering) the failed bank from the market, recovering as much as possible from the competitive sale and wind down of the operating businesses and financial and real estate assets of the company—so as to distribute as much proceeds as possible, in due order, to the most senior credit holders, then to the junior and finally (if anything is left) to the subordinated debts and equity holders.

Unlike liquidation, the resolution process is instead aimed at preserving the bank as a going concern—with clear differences in terms of prerequisites, objectives and tools:

- As for the application of the resolution mechanism, the bank would need to be in a situation of financial hardship, with current or potential strong liquidity crisis and or serious regulatory violations—e.g. available capital below the minimum regulatory threshold, but also serious governance issues and/or criminal activities that are suggesting the resolution of the bank—a most recent and notorious case regards BSI, the private bank finally being bought by EFG, that was asked by the Swiss Regulators to be "dissolved" after the merger because of allegedly serious frauds related to money laundering. There should also be, for the application of the resolution regime, no obvious market solution available and a clear and strong public interest to preserve the entity (including the case of reducing the overall costs of the intervention, vis a vis the utilization of the insurance deposit funds). For the liquidation, the main prerequisites would still regard things like serious imbalances between assets and liabilities, or significant losses that have caused a sizeable reduction of the bank's own funds, or the lack or disappearance of the legal prerequisites of the bank to operate as such. But it would also be clear that the preservation of public interest comes first and foremost (whatever that means… including the social and political implications potentially related to the default of the bank and its media coverage). Otherwise the markets can be let to absorb the liquidation of the bank without major troubles or systemic risks;

- Consistently with the prerequisites, the objectives of the resolution mechanism would then pursue the continuity of key, essential services (e.g. the "utility" functions performed by the bank, such as facilitating the payments and settlements process in the economy), and the avoidance of any negative repercussions or of major dislocations in the markets. The resolution would also seek to protect the "stakeholders" of the bank, avoiding a too traumatic liquidation play, that could cause, for example, losses of tens of thousands of jobs, or the collapse of local economies or of the real estate sector or of specific communities (in case the failed bank is dominant is its core territories), whilst minimizing the public finance intervention and the direct costs to taxpayers. The liquidation would instead pursue as a main objective the outright elimination of the bank from the market as an entity, guarantying the orderly conclusion (or wind down) of all existing contracts and relationships of the bank—still some partial sale of business areas or service functions "in going concern continuity" could be part of the liquidation;
- Finally, a different set of tools are also utilized for the resolution and liquidation procedures, and given the very different end state of "going concern" (for the resolution) and "gone concern" for the liquidation. For the resolution, a capital raise would be the most obvious tool, followed or accompanied by asset disposal (financial assets, either performing or NPL, and non-core operating companies), carve outs and M&A (including merger with a stronger bank), etc. Also, the creation of a "bridge bank", as temporary solution to keep the operating company afloat till a final solution is found, is often used, as it is the split of the failed bank into a "good" and a "bad bank" (or "non-core", as it is often called: with NPL and other loss making businesses which are just not viable for short term restructuring and recovery). For the liquidation, asset disposals are also usually employed along with, more often, winding down processes, aimed at speeding up the recovery of the proceeds that will be available for the partial reimbursements of the credit holders of the bank, and given their different hierarchy of seniority.

All in all, as mentioned in the beginning, resolution and liquidation procedures are more and more used as complementary approaches to address very complex situations, particularly in the case of distressed global banking groups owning a number of different legal entities and businesses across Countries, and whose final end state could be a mix of going and gone concern, and with the pains and burdens to be shared across multiple jurisdictions and with the relatives procedures requiring the agreement of many different regulators. It should also not be underestimated the implications of the "who is footing the bill" issue, should a global SIFI go down, as multiple insolvency regimes and deposit funds guarantees would come into play from different regions.

4.5 Capital Ratio and the "Bail In", from Tax Payers to Deposit Holders

In the old world where banks could not be allowed to fail, either because too big, or too relevant for their utilities functions, or because of their unmanageable political implications, given the potential knock down effect on the Country's economic cycle, and on the political election cycle caused by many, hungry stakeholders, the rule of the game was the "bail out". Should any bank behave in a reckless way, the State would have been ultimately ready to step in, and provide some stop loss guarantee to current shareholders, a full guarantee to debtholders.

In such situations, the State would also have ensured a last resort help in recapitalizing the operating company that would have, alternatively, capsized, bringing with it a good chunk of the relevant business counterparts—other banks included—that is now not the case anymore, with the most recent "Atlante fund", set up and funded by the largest and most capitalized Italian banks (even if following the moral suasion of the Italian Ministry of Finance and Economics and of the Bank of Italy) in order to ensure a back stop solution to the failed IPOs of a couple of medium sized banks (BP Vicentina and Veneto Banca) that failed the SREP testing of the ECB and had to close a regulatory capital gap—in any way—to avoid the alternative paths of resolution and liquidation.

In the past, the "bail out" of the State was ensured in a number of ways, from the direct State intervention (via the recapitalization of the failed banks, or the unlimited insurance of new bonds issued to refinance their balance sheet, or the creation and capitalization/full guarantee of a "bad bank", with all troubled loans and other financial assets, to be bought from the ailing bank at an above market/near book value price with taxpayers money), to the—indirectly operated—providential M&A executed by a stronger counterpart and with the help of the moral suasion of the main regulatory bodies of the relevant Country (Central Bank mainly).

This "bailing out" procedure, as we have seen, have created a number of distortions in the global financial system, allowing for an unlevelled playing field (the banks from stronger and more "provident" Countries—such as Germany—being able to better enjoy the stronger protection of the State vis a vis, say, Greek banks), moral hazards (not just on the side of the reckless bankers eager to take on even more risks, knowing that a safety net will in any case be present; but also on the side of the creditors, keen to lend to the riskier banks, as they tend to pay higher interest rates, and will be saved by the State anyway) and, finally a significant cost to taxpayers, that will end up footing a big bill, if things go really wrong.

The “bail in” procedure was then introduced as an alternative to ensure an orderly resolution of a banking failure with a view of significantly limit the potential requirements of public funds. In fact, following this procedure, during a bank’s resolution phase, the temporary administrator could use the bail-into:

- Recapitalize the bank to allow this to continue its operations (“open bank bail in”);
- Capitalize the “bridge bank” (“closed bank bail in”)—a third party bank temporarily authorized to hold the assets and liabilities of the insolvent bank—and charged with continuing the operations of the insolvent bank, until the bank becomes solvent again through the acquisition of another entity or through a successful liquidation.

The recapitalization/capitalization of the failed banks will then be used to:

- Write down or wipe out the value of the stock and of other quasi-capital instruments, starting from preferred shares to subordinated and convertible debts (please note that, as a partial application of the “bail in” procedures, the write down and potential full wipe out of subordinated debts instruments is also called “burden sharing”);
- Convert to stock and write down all other “plain vanilla” debt instruments, from the most junior to the most senior, following the red to green cascade represented in Fig. 4.3.

The graphical representation of the bail-in rule is then shown in Fig. 4.3—the hierarchy cascade.

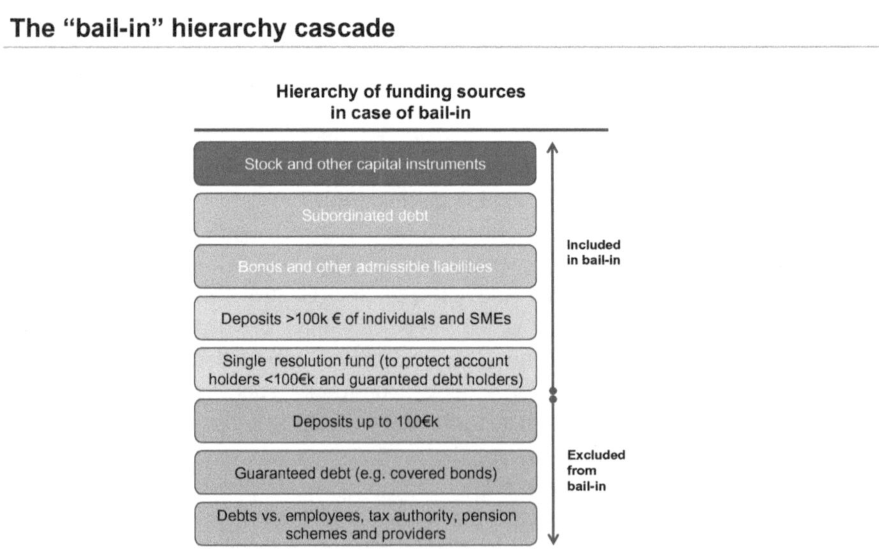

Fig. 4.3 The “bail-in” hierarchy cascade

The "bail in" rule, introduced fully into Law since January 1st 2016, has been aimed at avoiding moral hazard by shareholders (if not bank managers, that should become more worried of their decisions) and a greater scrutiny and continuous monitoring from the side of debt holders. Also (and mainly), it has been introduced in response to the angry taxpayers, tired of footing the bills driven by banks' failures, all too common and widespread since the beginning of the global financial crisis of 2008. Finally, the "bail in rule" has been aimed at improving the overall governance and management transparency of banks, even in times of failure, allocating the bank's losses in line with the bankruptcy law that would be applicable to any other kind of corporate of other industries.

The application of the "bail in" rule has however seen two earlier precedents to its adoption and full transformation into Law, starting from the meltdown of most of the Cyprus banking system (that caused the forced conversion and wipe out of a good share of the deposits of the banks of that Country), to the following failure of four local banks in Italy. In this second and more recent case, whilst the relevant authorities rushed at the end of 2015 to avoid the full application of the "bail in" rule, the "burden sharing" principle was however applied to the owners of subordinated debts, both Institutional investors and individuals—almost 50 % of this subordinated debts were placed to retail clients—causing a significant media backlash, with negative publicity going not only to the (then failed) originating banks, but also to the local regulators and government in charge.

The more general application of the "full bail in" procedure was then averted by the recapitalization of the four banks by the local resolution fund, managed by the Bank of Italy and financed by the local banking system, as the four banks were not among the ones already supervised by the ECB. The structured used, as shown in Fig. 4.4, had to face aggregated losses stemming from the insolvent banks of Euro 1.8 Bln circa.

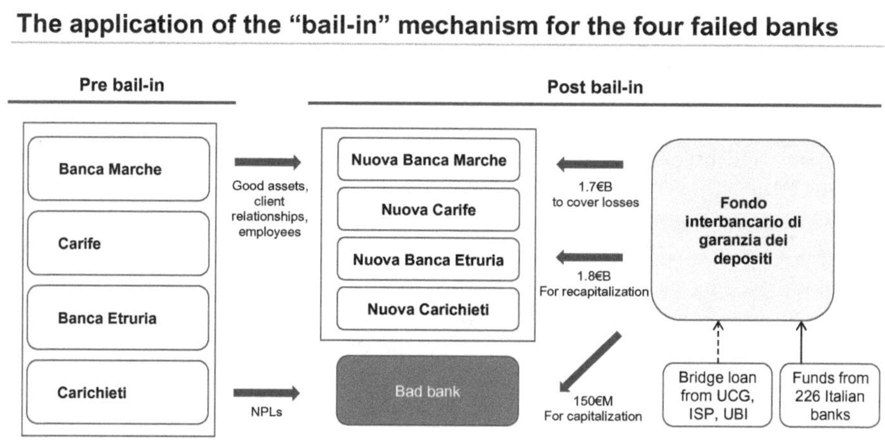

Fig. 4.4 The "resolution" of the four failed Italian banks

NPLs were then transferred to a "bad bank", also funded by the Italian banking system and run by the Bank of Italy, with a view of recovering or selling them in the market in the coming years via a competitive procedure run by REV (a servicing company owned by the Bank of Italy), whilst the good assets, the client relationships and the employees were transferred to the new banks. The "new banks" are four independent entities with no Legal/financial direct relationships with the previous institutions, that would also be managed for a quick sale via a competitive process to recover most of the capital injected to cover the losses and provide a minimum starting capital with a core T1 of almost 10 %. A more comprehensive discussion of the case of Banca Marche, the major of the four failed banks, is then provided in the following paragraph, with a graphical representation shown in Fig. 4.4—the resolution of the four failed Italian banks.

4.6 Banca Marche: The Origins of Its Demise

The second half of the '90s was a very busy time for banks in Italy, as a first wave of mergers was starting to consolidate and reshape the national banking landscape, traditionally fragmented and characterized by high level of inefficiencies and limited competitiveness. The most prominent outcome of that era was the creation of Unicredit, born in 1998 from the merger of several local banks under the unified governance of Unicredit and Credito Italiano. On a much smaller scale, Banca Marche was also a product of the same consolidation phase, as it was born in 1994 from the merger of the 150 years old CariPesaro and CariMa. Three years later it merged with two other smaller institutions, starting its journey towards growth and business diversification.

The diversification of its business and related services kept unfolding in the first half of the years 2000, with the creations in 2004 of a brokerage company in Luxembourg and of a leasing company in Italy. The bank at this time had about 250 branches in central Italy and assets for Euro 12.7 Bln, and was ready to take full advantage of the mildly positive economic cycle in his relevant regions of presence to grow its business, particularly in the real estate sector (as financing of real estate developers). In the years between 2004 and 2008 (the start of the financial crisis), both assets and revenues grew by 50 %, while net profits skyrocketed more than 500 %.

During these years, the bank's risk policies appeared already fairly aggressive, despite not being obviously worrying: provisions for credit risks remained flat while assets increased by half and, at a time when regulatory capital was less of a priority and much less under scrutiny, Banca Marche kept a Tier 1 ratio constantly below 7 % (whilst today Basel 3 has an 8 % "hard limit" and Banca d'Italia often uses its moral suasion to keep the banks under its direct supervision at least at a 10–11 % Tier 1 ratio level, at the times a 5–6 % was deemed enough). It could then be safely assumed that during those years the representation in the financial statements of the bank of what was really the quality of its assets was somehow optimistic—

particularly for its leasing real estate portfolio, and that the flat 6 % NPL rate may have been understating the real and more worrying state of the bank's loans—with specific reference to the loans to real estate developers. It was however just after the bursting of the global financial crisis in 2008 that the strange (and critical) situation of the bank became more apparent and urgent—setting the scene for the bank's tumultuous ending.

During the first years of the crisis, Banca Marche seemed able to keep cruising the markets at a speedier pace. Its assets and revenues kept growing steadily, albeit at a slower pace than before, increasing about 20 % between 2008 and 2011. The net income was also trending positively, while provisions for credit losses stayed steady at around Euro 130 Mil per year. All this lasted until 2012, the year when Banca d'Italia ended the bank's apparently uneventful and profitable sailing during an inspection, making clear of a situation that had become, to the eyes of bank's restructuring experts, all too common. It very easy, in banking, to be able to keep growing assets and revenues, at least in the short run, and even more so when a global crisis hits the markets.

Higher growth is in fact a kind of necessity for "zombie" banks that are off-setting an increasing cost of risk with the higher revenues coming from an even higher growth in lending assets (and higher net interest margins, if the new loans are increasingly going to more and more risky counterparts)—the cost of risk of a new, risky loans tends in fact to hit the bank's P&L just several months, if not years, ahead.

Still, in such a situation it becomes even easier to get to a point of no return, when the cost of risks of the aggressively accumulated loans becomes just unmanageable and a huge write off is then forcing the bank to declare a major loss and a significant wipe out of its regulatory capital base. The day or reckoning was thus long overdue and the Bank of Italy just helped in unveiling the real situation of the poor state of the bank.

4.7 Banca Marche: The Build up to Its Final Fall

The inspection in 2012 was not the first one made by Banca d'Italia to Banca Marche, that at that time was one of the top-20 banks in Italy: previous controls had happened in 2006, 2008, 2010 and 2011. None of those found major irregularities though … until 2012. The 2012 inspection found in fact serious irregularities in the accounting of non-performing loans, resulting in extra provisions for more than a billion Euro. In 2012 alone, 10 % of the whole credit portfolio was reclassified from "in bonis" to non-performing, bringing the overall NPL ratio to 25 % and turning the year's financial statement, considered in the black until June, to a net loss of more than Euro 500 Mln. The tier 1 ratio of the bank sunk consequently to about 5.5 %, and that even after a capital increase of Euro 180 Mln in the same year, completed through the issuance of new shares.

Initially, Banca d'Italia took a softer approach to turning the bank around: besides forcing the write-offs of the bad loans, it pushed for the resignation of Massimo Bianconi, the then General Manager of the company, later indicted with criminal conspiracy with the purpose of theft. It also imposed to the board members significant fines for irregularities, and required the above mentioned capital increase. But it was not until August 2013, five months after the publication of the 2012 financial statement, that Banca d'Italia decided that it was necessary to take a more decisive action and put the bank under temporary administration.

This decision was made all the more urgent and required by the results of the first half of 2013, that saw additional losses for more than Euro 230 Mln. due to provisions greater than twice that amount. The purpose of the temporary administration was to serve as a bridge period to find Euro 400 Mln circa from current or new shareholders to recapitalize the capital-depleted institution. The Board of Directors had to step down and two temporary administrators were appointed by the Central Bank. In the meanwhile, the president and vice-president of the bank (Lauro Costa and the influential Michele Ambrosini) had resigned. Oddly enough, just a few months later, Costa, soon-to-be convicted for thefts related to the bad management of the bank, received the title of Knight of the Republic, for his alleged merits at the helm of Banca Marche.

Unfortunately, during the temporary administration, neither new investors nor the existing foundations were willing or able to invest more capital into the struggling bank.

Considering the failure of the temporary administration, Banca Marche was then put under the stricter status of compulsory administration ("commissariamento") in October 2013. It was the 8th bank and largest forced into compulsory administration by Banca d'Italia in 2013, reaching a total of 12 banks with the same status. Again, the focus of the compulsory administration was the improvement of the capital ratios of the bank, as the two special commissioners, Terrinoni and Feliziani, announced the target to find about Euro 600 Mln of fresh capital.

Banks under compulsory administration do not publish regular balance sheet, and the transparency on the results of the compulsory administration appears far from ideal. However, it became apparent through time that it was not successful, and it was not possible to maintain the bank as a going concern. Two years later, after using all the time legally available to try to save Banca Marche, Banca d'Italia and the Italian Treasury Department gave up, and included the financial institution in a list of 4 Italian banks to be subject to the "burden sharing", a resolution procedure recently introduced by new EU banking regulations, but still avoiding the full application of the "bail in"—something that would have become inevitable just few weeks later, from January 1st 2016.

The other three institutions were Carife, Carichieti and Banca Popolare dell'Etruria (particularly this last one), had just sold a massive amount of subordinated debts to its retail clients—individuals and families, mostly mass market, and often in neglect of the basic interest of its customers, not to mention the prevailing laws on asset gathering and management for non-Institutional, non-professional clients.

4.8 The Resolution and Final "Burden Sharing"

In mid 2014, the European Commission approved then the Banking Recovery and Resolution directive (BRRD). This directive provides National authorities with more comprehensive and effective capabilities and procedures to deal with failing banks at national level. The directive became then effective from the beginning of 2015.

Among the purposes of the newly introduced recovery procedures, there was the limitation of government intervention to "bail out" banks with capital shortage, introducing the concept of "bail in", i.e. the allocation of losses of the failing institution according to bankruptcy law, while maintaining the bank as a going concern.

In addition to this, the BRRD introduced the creation of national "single resolution funds", managed at Country level, that collects contributions from all banks belonging to the system (as a percentage of deposits), and whose purpose is to provide a further capital "cushion" in case of a bank failure.

The case of Banca Marche and of the other 3 Italian banks was the first to see the application of the "bail in" procedure. It was not the first banking crisis being managed at government level in 2015, as for instance Portugal poured between 2 and 3 billion euros in the bail-out of Banco Internacional de Funchal, but it was the first instance in which, allegedly, the European Central Bank imposed the utilization of an (albeit partial, and limited to the application of the new rule to the subordinated debts) bail in procedure, not without controversy in Italy.

The bail in for the four Italian bank was then managed as a single operation, i.e. jointly coordinated for all of the 4 banks. The aggregated losses to be covered were about 1.7 € billions (with a larger hole for Banca Marche versus what was present 2 years earlier). The solution that was engineered included three separate components:

- All the core assets of the four banks were transferred to four new entities, called respectively "New Banca Marche", "New Carife" etc. Their balance sheet included deposits, client relationships, employees, loans "in bonis", real estate. During this step, the value of all shares of the old banks was zeroed, and convertible bonds were also wiped out (for a total loss of about Euro 430 Mln). Senior bonds were instead honored. The four "new" banks continued to operate in place of the old legal entities, without interruption of service. The newly injected capital for the new entities was about Euro 1.8 Mln, coming from the new Italian Resolution Fund, managed by the resolution arm of Banca d'Italia;
- All non-performing loans were then transferred under the same "bad bank" (but still kept segregated. These loans at this point were largely written off (with a net book value of 18 % circa), so that a minimal capitalization was required. The bad bank purchased the loans at market price from the old banks. The total face value of the loans transferred to the bad bank was Euro 8.5 Bln circa, and the related capitalization of the bad bank was put equal to Euro 150 Mln circa, plus Euro 500 Mln raised as further guaranteed funding from the main banks of the system;

- All five entities (the four new banks and the bad bank) were placed under the control of a "resolution authority" and related fund, managed by Banca d'Italia, that has the purpose to extract the maximum value from the assets, finding acquirers for the new, cleaned up banks and for the bad bank (to be either sold—as a whole or as a collection of selected assets—to third party specialized players, or to be serviced by professional credit recovery agencies to collect the maximum possible amount). The funding of the Italian resolution fund came from the national banking system: almost Euro 4 Bln overall, of which Euro 2 Bln as a short term bridge loan by Intesa Sanpaolo, Unicredit and UBI Banca, to be then reattributed to the overall banking system; and a further Euro 2 Bln as a long term loan by the same banks, to be repaid with the proceeds of the sale of the new banks and of the bad bank. The management of the five new entities was assigned by Bank of Italy to the former General Manager of Unicredit, Roberto Nicastro, who started then to manage a competitive sale.

As the sale process of the four good banks and of the bad bank unfold, few questions could be considered at the light of the narrative described so far, at given the potential outcomes of the sale.

More specifically, was the failure of Banca Marche avoidable at all? And when was the point of no return overcome? Was the failure of the medium sized regional bank a consequence of its poor governance, and related mismanagement (with potential frauds still being investigated by the local authority?). Or of its business model, too much driven by growth and diversification, even at a time when the credit cycle was negatively reversing? And what about its overreliance on the local economy of the Marche region? And what about its big bet on real estate developers—doing business outside its core area?

Once the bank started then to clearly show its insolvent status, was the administration process, in its different stages, effective and efficient, if not in recovering the going concern (as several attempted sale processes failed) at least in preserving the remaining value for the stakeholders? Or was the capital gap just increasing by the day, with the extraordinary administration just buying time before the final day of reckoning? How would it have played, without the new BRRD? And, given the new table of the new Laws, was the intervention in the late fall of 2015 the best possible strategy, and with what consequences?

Going then to the spring of 2016, with the two sales processes, for the good banks and for the bad bank, undergoing, how would the best outcome turn out to be, for the Italian banking system and for the good banks specifically?

Would they be better off ending up owned by private equity funds, or by other traditional banking players? And, specifically, on which basis and for which stakeholders (clients, employees, local communities etc.) we could argue they would be better off, and why? And finally, what should have been done and how their crisis should have been managed, following instead our "bankaround" approach—using all the four levers of the RTX2 approach, from restructuring and resolution, to turnaround and transformation?

4.9 Conclusion: The Bankaround to Come

We have been arguing, from the beginning of this book, that a profound change is happening right now in the financial services industry, and that this will lead massive "creative destruction", maybe—but not necessarily—for the benefit of Fin Tech challengers, able to surf the opportunities coming from the digital innovation, but also to navigate just outside the increasingly more troubled waters of the regulatory and compliance realms.

We have also examined, albeit at an high level, the main discontinuities and disruptions taking shape for most of the major fundamental functions of the GFS, and the potential, methodological but also empirical approach that could "hold water" in its navigation of the restructuring and turnaround, not to mention resolution and transformation challenges that have for too long been avoided or postponed, in the continental European banking sector particularly. As we move towards unchartered water, few obvious questions still remains unaddressed:

- Will the incumbent, traditional banks have a chance at all to prosper and keep growing (assuming most of them will survive for a number of years anyway, because of all kind of systemically important reasons, still strong commercial franchise and very patient and affectionate shareholders)? And which characteristics should they possess, in order to have better chances to make it?
- Will then the banks' top management be able to do it, leading the change, with the current set of skills—technical knowledge and managerial experience—and embedded culture—as a mix of core value, approach to change, emotional intelligence and attitude towards difficult decisions and actions?

We have left with open questions the few case studies presented in this handbook, and the future "bankaround" to come surely does not deserve to be treated differently. However, as a stimulus for future discussion and academic analysis and, more importantly, for future action and managerial testing "on the battle field", we want to suggest some initial hypothesis for elaboration—potentially leading to some "good enough" competitive invariances that are good in times of crisis, even if not absolutely true for any phase of the economic cycle.

Starting from the "bank with the greatest change of making it", we would suggest considering the following:

- Creation follows transparency and the recognition of truth. The banks that have the greatest chances to make it are therefore the ones ready to be honest with themselves, and face the bare facts and the inevitably tough truths. The more time is wasted before recognizing an issue and declaring this openly even from an accounting and regulatory point of view, the more real economic value is wasted in the process, not to mention the credibility and reputation of the bank and of the industry in general. This is clearly a challenge for most banks that cannot face the challenge of a "fully transparent" balance sheet, as it is of the regulators and watchdogs themselves (not to mention the policy makers and the politicians) that are still allowing this bad or suboptimal practices, even if formally supported by accounting or regulation rules (albeit, following a very stretched interpretation sometimes at odds with reality);

- Creation is then better reignited from a clean slate. The banks that are more effective in being able to put themselves back onto a clean slate kind of situation have the greatest chances of doing a better job. If a past investment was lousy, or has just become surpassed by the current environment, better to recognize it, and declare as sunk cost what is really sunk, and as a write off what is really un-useful and un-recoverable, to say the least. A lot has been told on the social role of banks to protect the employment, the community and the overall stakeholders—even the society at times. But truth is that banks were not born (at least are not supposed now) to do work for non-profit purposes, that is wasting the money of their shareholders. And actually, keeping a bank inefficient, e.g. refusing to reduce the excess number of employees it has got, means wasting resources, and allocating them in suboptimal ways, thus arming the overall wealth creation potential of the ecosystem in which they live. A credit allocation not done on the pure basis of economic merit will create much more harm than letting some companies to starve; and thus forcing them out of business, it their business is just not good enough to repay a loan, will create more value in the mid-term than just trying to help them all, or procrastinate the nasty decision to take. Consistently, keeping redundant, not productive workers in the work force of the bank will mean creating less fractions with the Unions and with their community in the short run, but at the expense of their options to find a more rewarding job (for their employer and for them as well), and for sure at the expenses of the shareholders of the bank, maybe of its debtholders and even of its customers if these oversized workforce is just translating in more bureaucracy, internal meddling and lousy service;
- Creation needs to be consistent with the prevailing ecosystem—whatever this will be. Dinosaurs were the strongest until (probably) a comet hit the planet, but then they just had to cease to exist. Therefore, if the prevailing ecosystem is inevitably going towards the digitalization of most of the investment and consumption decisions, traditional banks need to take stock and radically alter their business model, not just modifying it, step by step, taking out a new layer every year, as with the proverbial onion (that will ultimately make you cry). Decision making should therefore be, in fact, "decisive", with particular regard to target business and operating models design and positioning—basing its conclusion on an objective recognition of the prevailing state of the ecosystem—most likely a moving target for many years to come, therefore requiring even more proactivity in managing it and the transformation required from the bank's side. On the other side, regulators should also help, if not in easing, at least in not constraining the room of maneuver required for banks to change. Current regulators are in fact apparently forcing the dinosaurs to stay put and get more rigid and fat as they see the comet arrive;
- Creation is based as much on destruction as on development. Banks that will most likely make it will be good at quickly, effectively, relentlessly and sometimes even ruthlessly destroy what needs to be liquidated, but also at

cunningly rebuilding, or developing anew whatever the future best prevailing business will chose to target. As good value creators could be good cost cutters, but exceptional ones should also be good in creating new sources of revenues and growth, with lower risks involved and better value delivered to customers in competitive markets, maybe two sets of very different people are in need for banks to execute this "pars destruens" and "pars construens" strategy. Beware therefore of banks that are restructuring their way out of a crisis just by de-leveraging, slashing costs and exiting non-core businesses: that is the easy way to take out fat, but you then need to rebuild muscles, to be competitive in the new arena, and ultimately it is healthy growth—a much harder target to get—that can drive the success of an organization or living species, and then profitability.

From a managerial and leadership and "people management" point of view, few considerations could follow, often against the most common prevailing views:

- The leader of a "bankaround" (and not just of a phase of it, be it resolution, restructuring, turn around or transformation) will need to have a complete view of the world, with a set of very heterogeneous set of skills and experiences. The "ultimate heads chopper" may be good for some part of the restructuring; and the "performance improver" may be good for some of the following phases; as well as the great "cash manager" and the great "liquidator" that could do miracles in a resolution, or at least for a portion of it; and the "creative visionary" could held designing the perfect business and operating model transformation to be. But the great "bankaround leader" will need to be a bit of both, at the same time, or be able to be a different kind of manager at different times, as she/he may also have to master the pragmatic view of an entrepreneur, the financial skills of an investment banker, the industrial knowledge of a management consultant, the gut feeling of a principal investor and, of course, the good common sense and managerial passion of a top manager of a bank—and managing different experts through time, keeping some balance among all these different set of objectives and trade-offs in the back of his mind;
- The leader of a "bankaround" will then need to be ready and feel at ease in facing the unknown and the unpredictable and be quick in taking decision and hands on in getting on to actions execution, but all the times just remembering that her/his view is not perfect and should not even aspire to be. In restructuring it can be good enough being right 60 % of the time, and in turn around 70 % and in transformation 80 %. It may even be good to be 55 % right in resolution—provided you do something, effectively and quickly—as sometimes even the perception of inaction could be fatal to the good part of the company, and fatal it is for most of the value that will definitely migrate away from the bank. As the leader of the "bankaround" will struggle to survive every single week at first, and then months and then quarter and maybe semester, it will need to have the courage and the persistence, and still the love for the adventure of the great

warrior, general, politician, traveler… and its irony, as the last defense from her/his otherwise uncontrollable, growing and potentially very dangerous, and already obviously "bigger than life" ego—she/he will need to be able to put everything into perspective.

In one of our previous handbook, written almost 20 years ago, we wrote of the leader of the winning banks that had to face the value creation challenge and the new competitive environment of a finally liberalized sector as the Ulysses navigating her/his organization beyond the last known waters, into the open ocean.

And we clarified we thought of two Ulysses, when thinking of this: the one of Omer—courageous, risk taker, quick to decide and smart, and fearless in acting and often ruthlessly; and the one of Joyce—looking at the facts of life with an ironic view, shaken by the events, still standing, and heroic in the un-eventful circumstances as in the epic ones. Two very different Ulysses, for two very different managerial stiles—still in need to be co-existing. Even more today, with the "bankaround" challenges to come, we feel the winning leader will need to be the two Ulysses, navigating in the unknown, deep, wide and full of dangers Ocean.

Bibliography

King M (2016) The end of alchemy: money, banking and the future of the global economy. W. W. Norton and Company, New York
Scardovi C (2014) Industrializzare la banca. EGEA, Utrecht
Scardovi C (2015) Credit work out holistic active management. Springer, Berlin
Scardovi C, Bezzecchi A (2014) Banking e Real Estate. EGEA, Utrecht

C. Scardovi, *Restructuring and Innovation in Banking*,
SpringerBriefs in Finance, DOI 10.1007/978-3-319-40204-8

Kolibri 360 GmbH
Ferdinand-Jühlke-Straße 7
99095 Erfurt, Deutschland
produktsicherheit@kolibri360.de